P9-DXS-879

Table of Contents

Unit 1: Music Basics and Black Keys
Keeping the Hands Fit 6
Technic Exercise 1: **Warm-Ups Away from
the Keyboard** 6
Technic Exercise 2: **Warm-Ups Away from
the Keyboard** 7
Deep Breathing 7
How to Sit at the Piano 8
Hand Position 8
Four Good Reasons for Playing with Curved Fingers .9
Technic Exercise: **Away from the Keyboard** 9
Finger Numbers 10
Practice Exercise: **Away from the Keyboard** 10
Piano Tones 11
Dynamic Signs 11
Using a Good Curved Hand Position 11
The Keyboard 12
The Damper Pedal 12
Playing 2-Black-Key Groups 13
Playing 3-Black-Key Groups 13
Quarter Note 14
Rhythm Exercise: **Away from the Keyboard** 14
Technic Exercise: **Away from the Keyboard** 14
Quarter Rest 15
Rhythm Exercise: **Away from the Keyboard** 15
Playing 2-Black-Key Groups Going Up and Down . . .15
Half Note 16
Rhythm Exercise: **Away from the Keyboard** 16
Technic Exercise: Warm-Ups on 3-Black-Key Groups 16
Half Rest 17
Rhythm Exercise: **Away from the Keyboard** 17
Playing 3-Black-Key Groups Going Up and Down . . .17
Hands Together on Both Black-Key Groups 18
Amazing Grace 🔊 (1*) 18
Alouette 🔊 (2) 18
Tom Dooley 🔊 (3) 19

Unit 2: White Keys
Playing White Keys 20
Written Exercise: **Away from the Keyboard** 21
Dotted Half Note 22
Rhythm Exercise: **Away from the Keyboard** 22
C-D-E Groups 22
Whole Note 24
Rhythm Exercise: **Away from the Keyboard** 24
F-G-A-B Groups 24
Whole Rest 24
Written Exercise: **Away from the Keyboard** 26
Time Signature 27

Rhythm Exercise: **Away from the Keyboard** 27
Left Hand C Position 28
Technic Exercise: **Left Hand Warm-Ups** 28
Right Hand C Position 29
Technic Exercise: **Right Hand Warm-Ups** 29
Ode to Joy (Beethoven) 🔊 (4) 30
Aura Lee 🔊 (5) 31

Unit 3: The Staff
The Treble Clef Sign 32
Written Exercise: **Away from the Keyboard** 32
The Bass Clef Sign 32
Written Exercise: **Away from the Keyboard** 32
Line Notes and Space Notes 33
Written Exercise: **Away from the Keyboard** 33
The Bass Clef 34
Written Exercise: **Away from the Keyboard** 34
Write and Play Exercise 34
The Treble Clef 35
Written Exercise: **Away from the Keyboard** 35
Write and Play Exercise 35
The Grand Staff 36
C Position on the Grand Staff 36
Write and Play Exercise 36
Written Exercise: **Away from the Keyboard** 37
Write and Play Exercise 37
Lightly Row 37
Sight Reading Made Easy—Part 1 38
Stepping Along 🔊 (6) .38
Practice Exercise: Sight Reading 38
Sight Reading Made Easy—Part 2 39
Skipping Along 🔊 (7) .39
The Repeat Sign 39
Mexican Hat Dance 🔊 (8) 39

Unit 4: Melodic and Harmonic Intervals
Melodic Intervals 40
2nds 40
Seconds 🔊 (9) 40
3rds 41
Thirds 🔊 (10) 41
Au Claire de la Lune 🔊 (11) 41
Tisket, a Tasket 🔊 (12) 42
Practice Exercise: Sight Reading 42
Write and Play Exercise 43
Harmonic Intervals 44
Rockin' Intervals 🔊 (13) 44
More Harmonic 2nds and 3rds 45
Harmonica Rock 🔊 (14) 45
Melodic 4ths and 5ths 46

*CD/GM track number

4ths 46
Fourths 🔊 (15) .46
5ths 47
Fifths 🔊 (16) 47
Rock Along! 🔊 (17) 47
Good King Wenceslas 🔊 (18) 48
My Fifth 🔊 (19) .48
Write and Play Exercise 49
Harmonic 4ths and 5ths 50
Jingle Bells 🔊 (20) 50
More Harmonic 4ths and 5ths 51
Dueling Harmonics 🔊 (21) 51
Written Exercise: **Away from the Keyboard** 52
Interval Review 53
   Melodies 🔊 (22) 53
   Harmonies 🔊 (23) 53

Unit 5: Middle C Position
Middle C Position .54
Thumbs on C! 🔊 (24) 54
Camptown Races (Foster) 🔊 (25) 55
New Dynamic Signs *(crescendo, diminuendo)* 55
Surprise Symphony (Haydn) 🔊 (26) 55
Practice Exercise: Sight Reading 56
Written Exercise: **Away from the Keyboard** 57
Jolly Old Saint Nicholas 🔊 (27) 58
Eine Kleine Nachtmusik (Mozart) 🔊 (28) 59

Unit 6: Chords
C Major Chords for RH 60
C Major Chords for LH 60
Written Exercise: **Away from the Keyboard** 61
Brother John 🔊 (29) 62
Practice Exercise: Sight Reading 62
Here's a Happy Song 🔊 (30) 63
Practice Exercise: Sight Reading 63
B for Left Hand 64
C Major and G7 Chords for Left Hand 64
Written Exercise: **Away from the Keyboard** 65
Tied Notes 66
Merrily We Roll Along 🔊 (31) 66
Practice Exercise: Sight Reading 66
Largo (Dvořák) 🔊 (32) 67
Practice Exercise: Sight Reading 67
B for Right Hand 68
C Major and G7 Chords for Right Hand 68
Written Exercise: **Away from the Keyboard** 69
Practice Exercise: Sight Reading 70
Mary Ann 🔊 (33) 71

Unit 7: New Time Signature, More Chords
Time Signature (¾) 72
Rhythm Exercise: **Away from the Keyboard** 72

Rockets 🔊 (34) .72
Sea Divers 🔊 (35) 73
Slurs and Legato Playing 73
Practice Exercise: Sight Reading 73
Written Exercise: **Away from the Keyboard** 74
Rhythm Exercise: **Away from the Keyboard** 74
Write and Play Exercise 75
Day Is Done 75
Slurs and Ties 75
Down in the Valley 🔊 (36) 76
What Can I Share? 🔊 (37) 77
C Major and F Major Chords for Left Hand 78
Practice Exercise: Sight Reading 79
Written Exercise: **Away from the Keyboard** 80
Incomplete Measure 81
When the Saints Go Marching In
  (RH melody) 🔊 (38) 81
A for Right Hand 82
C Major and F Major Chords for Right Hand 82
Practice Exercise: Sight Reading 83
Written Exercise: **Away from the Keyboard** 84
When the Saints Go Marching In
  (LH melody) 🔊 (39) 85
Old Country Music 🔊 (40) 86

Unit 8: G Position, The Sharp Sign
G Position 88
Intervals in G Position 88
Write and Play Exercise 89
The Bandleader 89
Practice Exercise: Sight Reading 90
Love Somebody! 🔊 (41) 91
A Friend Like You 🔊 (42) 91
Sharp Sign 92
Money Can't Buy Ev'rything! 🔊 (43) 92
Write and Play Exercise 93
Practice Exercise: Sight Reading 94
Will You, Won't You? 🔊 (44) 95

Unit 9: Chords in G Position
G Major and D7 Chords for Left Hand 96
Practice Exercise: Sight Reading 97
The Cuckoo 🔊 (45) 98
Write and Play Exercise 99
Liza Jane 99
G Major and D7 Chords for Right Hand 100
Broken Chords and Block Chords 100
Practice Exercise: Sight Reading 101
Written Exercise: **Away from the Keyboard** . . .102
I Know Where I'm Goin' 🔊 (46) 103
The Damper Pedal 104
Practice Exercise: Sight Reading 104

BOOK 1

Play Piano Now!

Alfred's Basic Adult Piano Course

Lesson · Theory · Sight Reading · Technic

An Easy Beginning Method for Busy Adults

WILLARD A. PALMER • MORTON MANUS • E. L. LANCASTER

ISBN 0-7390-0764-5 (Book)
ISBN 0-7390-1454-4 (Book & CD)
ISBN 0-7390-1455-2 (CD)
ISBN 0-7390-1457-9 (GM Disk)

Alfred

Foreword

In a recent survey of adults, it was discovered that many wished they had studied piano when they were younger. They now regret not being able to perform and enjoy all the pleasures playing the piano can bring. The good news is that it is never too late to begin.

With *Play Piano Now!* busy adults can learn to play quickly and easily. Using favorite pieces and the popular conceptual core from *Alfred's Basic Adult Piano Course,* this all-new format allows for the gradual introduction of music fundamentals, followed by sufficient pages of reinforcement. Students can now progress steadily at a comfortable pace without having to repeat the same page again and again. The use of more pages on the same topic makes each practice session interesting and fresh, allowing for a thorough understanding of each subject before moving to something new.

One of the most important skills that adults must develop to insure long-term enjoyment of the piano is the ability to play at sight. Throughout the book are specially constructed *Sight Reading* exercises. These exercises use the same concepts as the related songs but are a little easier. Realizing that material can only be used for sight reading one time, the student should play these exercises once each day. The page should become a little easier each day as patterns become more familiar. At the lesson the student should play the exercise for the teacher without stopping, then discuss problems encountered during practice and at the lesson.

Also included in this new approach are *Technic* and *Write & Play* exercises, combined with appealing and familiar songs to perform. An added feature is specially marked exercises (*Writing* and *Rhythm*) that can be completed *Away from the Keyboard.* This feature will be extremely helpful for adults whose practice time is limited and who must take advantage of every free moment. There are even exercises for warming the hands before performing, to keep them flexible. Nothing has been left out. It's fun, it's easy, and it really works!

A General MIDI CD (19656) is available. It offers a full piano recording and background accompaniment for songs throughout the book identified by the following icon: 🔊 Playing along with the background accompaniment promotes musical enjoyment and rhythmic stability. Visit alfred.com to purchase MIDI files from this book.

The authors wish you much success in learning to play the piano. The possibilities are endless. Whether you perform for your own enjoyment or for a party of friends, you'll find that playing the piano is a gift you can give yourself that lasts for a lifetime!

Willard A. Palmer • **Morton Manus** • **E. L. Lancaster**

Harp Song 🔊 (47) 105
E for Left Hand 106
A New Position of the C Major Chord 106
Practice Exercise: Sight Reading 107
Write and Play Exercise .108
Practice Exercise: Technic 108
Beautiful Brown Eyes 🔊 (48) 109
E for Right Hand 110
New C Major Chord Position for Right Hand 110
Practice Exercise: Sight Reading 111
Alpine Melody 🔊 (49) 112
Written Exercise: **Away from the Keyboard** 113

**Unit 10: The Flat Sign, Eighth Notes,
        Dotted Quarter Notes**
Flat Sign 114
Rock It Away! 🔊 (50) .114
Practice Exercise: Sight Reading 115
Write and Play Exercise .116
Für Ludwig 🔊 (51) 117
Fermata 118
Shoo, Fly, Shoo! 🔊 (52) 118
Eighth Notes 119
Rhythm Exercise: **Away from the Keyboard** . . .119
Skip to My Lou 🔊 (53) 119
Rhythm Exercise: **Away from the Keyboard** . . .120
Practice Exercise: Sight Reading 120
Standing in the Need of Prayer 🔊 (54) 121
Combining Middle C Position and C Position 122
The Gift to Be Simple 🔊 (55) 122
Practice Exercise: Sight Reading 123
Technic Exercise: **Warm-Ups** 124
The Amazing Aerobics of Hanon
  No. 1 124
  No. 2 125
Dotted Quarter Notes 126
Rhythm Exercise: **Away from the Keyboard** . . .126
Measures from Familiar Songs
  Using Dotted Quarter Notes 127
Alouette 🔊 (56) 128
Rhythm Exercise: **Away from the Keyboard** . . .129
Practice Exercise: Sight Reading 129
Practice Exercise: Sight Reading 130
Ach, du lieber Augustine 🔊 (57) 131

Unit 11: 6ths, 7ths and Octaves
6ths 132
RH C Position plus 1 note (A) 132
LH C Position plus 1 note (A) 132
Technic Exercise: **Warm-Up** 133
Lavender's Blue 🔊 (58) 133
Write and Play Exercise .134

New Time Signature ($\frac{2}{4}$) 135
Kum-ba-yah! 🔊 (59) .135
Written Exercise: **Away from the Keyboard** . . .136
London Bridge 🔊 (60) 137
Michael, Row the Boat Ashore 🔊 (61) 137
Practice Exercise: Sight Reading 138
Blow the Man Down! 🔊 (62) 139
Moving Up and Down the Keyboard in 6ths 140
Staccato 140
Lone Star Waltz 🔊 (63) 140
Practice Exercise: Sight Reading 142
Hanon's Aerobic Sixths .143
Listen to the Mocking Bird 🔊 (64) 144
Written Exercise: **Away from the Keyboard** . . .145
7ths 146
Octaves 146
Practice Exercise: Sight Reading 147
Café Vienna 🔊 (65) 148
Lullaby 🔊 (66) 149
Index/Glossary of Terms and Symbols 150

Unit 1

Music Basics and Black Keys

Keeping the Hands Fit

Before practicing, it is good to soak the hands for a few minutes in warm water to promote circulation. Towel the hands vigorously until they are dry. Many concert pianists use warm water on their hands before beginning to play.

To keep your hands in the best condition for playing, practice the following exercises several times daily.

Technic Exercise 1: Warm-Ups Away from the Keyboard

A. Holding your arms in playing position, palms downward, *clench* both hands tightly, making two fists. Hold while you count "ONE-TWO."

make tight fists   *palms down*

B. *Snap* the fingers quickly outward, opening both hands. Do this with great vigor. Hold this position with all fingers extended. Count "THREE-FOUR."

snap fingers open   *palms down*

C. *Shake* out both hands, dangling from the wrists. Count "ONE-TWO-THREE-FOUR."

shake hands   *keep hands loose and relaxed*

Technic Exercise 2: Warm-Ups Away from the Keyboard

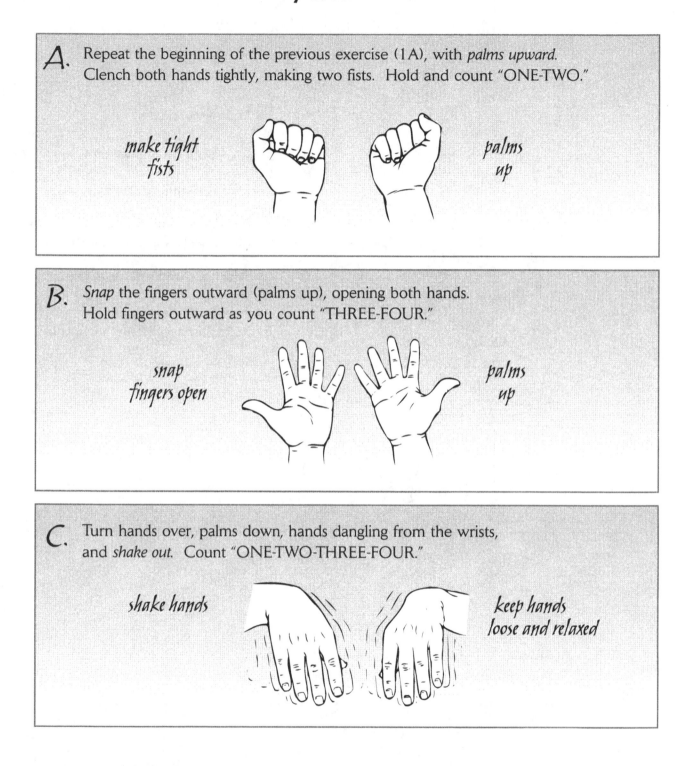

A. Repeat the beginning of the previous exercise (1A), with *palms upward.*
Clench both hands tightly, making two fists. Hold and count "ONE-TWO."

make tight fists   *palms up*

B. *Snap* the fingers outward (palms up), opening both hands.
Hold fingers outward as you count "THREE-FOUR."

snap fingers open   *palms up*

C. Turn hands over, palms down, hands dangling from the wrists,
and *shake out.* Count "ONE-TWO-THREE-FOUR."

shake hands   *keep hands loose and relaxed*

Deep Breathing

Warm-Up Exercises 1 and 2 may be combined with deep breathing by:

1. Breathing *in* (the lower abdomen moves outward) on examples 1A and 2A.

2. Breathing *out* (the lower abdomen moves inward) on examples 1B and 2B.

3. Breathing *in* on examples 1C and 2C while counting to four; then breathing *out* while counting to four, holding hands still and loose.

How to Sit at the Piano

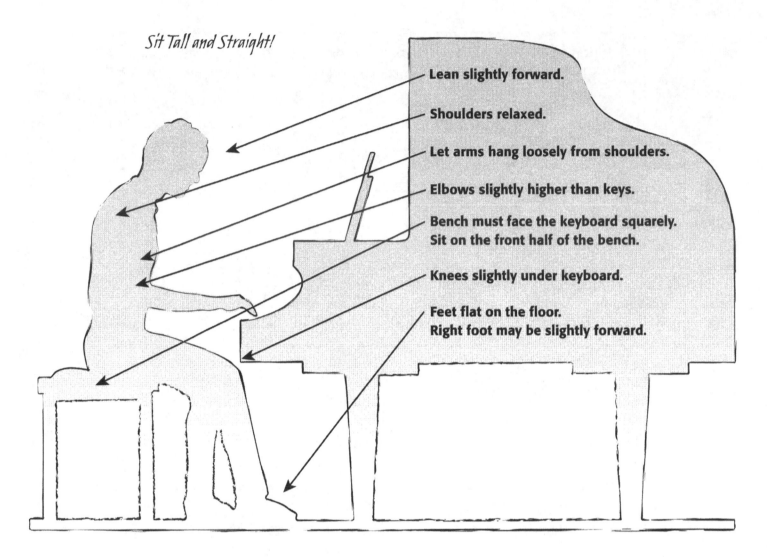

Sit Tall and Straight!

Lean slightly forward.

Shoulders relaxed.

Let arms hang loosely from shoulders.

Elbows slightly higher than keys.

Bench must face the keyboard squarely.
Sit on the front half of the bench.

Knees slightly under keyboard.

Feet flat on the floor.
Right foot may be slightly forward.

Hand Position

Curve your fingers when you play!
Pretend you have a bubble in your hand.
Hold the bubble gently, so it doesn't break!

Four Good Reasons for Playing with Curved Fingers

1. When the fingers are curved, each finger has, in effect, the same length.

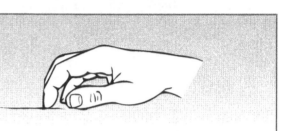

2. Curved fingers bring the thumb into the correct playing position.

3. With curved fingers, keys respond instantly. You are in control when you *curve!*

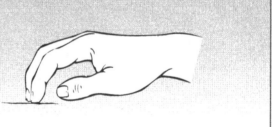

4. Moving over the keys will require turning the thumb *under* the fingers and crossing fingers *over* the thumb. Curved fingers provide an *"arch"* that makes this motion possible.

Very Important

Keep fingernails reasonably short.
It is impossible to curve fingers properly with long fingernails.

Technic Exercise: Away from the Keyboard

On a table top or other flat surface, practice curving the fingers on each hand for a good hand position. Do your hands look like the above illustrations?

Finger Numbers

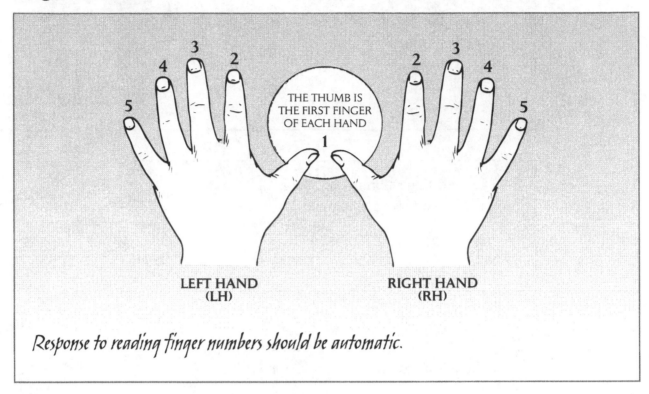

THE THUMB IS
THE FIRST FINGER
OF EACH HAND

LEFT HAND
(LH)

RIGHT HAND
(RH)

Response to reading finger numbers should be automatic.

Practice Exercise: Away from the Keyboard

Place both hands on a table top or other flat surface, curving the fingers. Practice tapping the fingers as indicated.

Tapping the *same* fingers	**Tapping the *opposite* fingers**
• Tap finger 1 with both hands.	• Tap LH finger 5 and RH finger 1.
• Tap finger 2 with both hands.	• Tap LH finger 4 and RH finger 2.
• Tap finger 3 with both hands.	• Tap LH finger 3 and RH finger 3.
• Tap finger 4 with both hands.	• Tap LH finger 2 and RH finger 4.
• Tap finger 5 with both hands.	• Tap LH finger 1 and RH finger 5.
Now tap the above in reverse order.	Now tap the above in reverse order.

Piano Tones

When you play a key, a hammer inside your piano touches a string to make a tone.
When you drop into a key with a *little* weight, you make a *soft* tone.
When you use *more* weight, you make a *louder* tone.

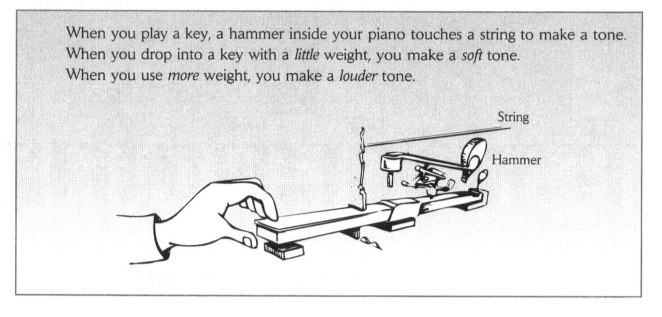

Dynamic Signs tell how loud or soft to play.

p *(piano)* = soft

mf *(mezzo forte)* = moderately loud

f *(forte)* = loud

Using a Good Curved Hand Position

1. Choose any white key and play it *piano* (*p*) with left hand finger 1,
followed by fingers 2, 3, 4 and 5 on the same key. Repeat with the right hand.

2. Choose any white key and play it *mezzo forte* (*mf*) with left hand finger 5,
followed by fingers 4, 3, 2 and 1 on the same key. Repeat with the right hand.

3. Choose any white key and play it *forte* (*f*) with left hand finger 3,
followed by 1, 5, 4 and 2 on the same key. Repeat with the right hand.

4. Choose any white key and play it several times with left hand finger 3, beginning
piano (*p*). Make each tone a little louder until you reach *mezzo forte* (*mf*); then
continue playing louder until you reach *forte* (*f*). Repeat with the right hand.

The Keyboard

The keyboard is made up of white keys and black keys.

The black keys are in groups of two's and three's.

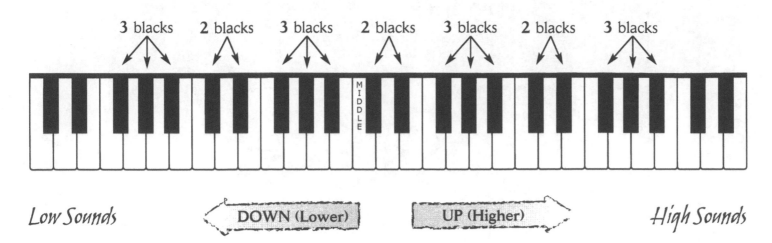

3 blacks   **2** blacks   **3** blacks   **2** blacks   **3** blacks   **2** blacks   **3** blacks

Low Sounds   DOWN (Lower)   UP (Higher)   *High Sounds*

On the keyboard, *down* is to the left, and *up* is to the right.

As you move left, the tones sound *lower.* As you move right, the tones sound *higher.*

The Damper Pedal

The *right* pedal is called the *damper pedal.*

When you hold the damper pedal down, any tone you sound will continue after you release the key.

Use the *right foot* on the damper pedal. Always keep your heel on the floor. Use your ankle like a hinge.

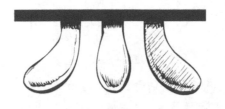

1. Find groups of 2 black keys high and low on the keyboard. Hold down the damper pedal as you play both keys at once, first with LH 2 and 3; then with RH 2 and 3.

2. Find groups of 3 black keys high and low on the keyboard. Hold down the damper pedal as you play all three keys at once, first with LH 2, 3 and 4; then with RH 2, 3 and 4.

Playing 2-Black-Key Groups

LH

1. Using LH 2 3, begin at the middle of the keyboard and play all the 2-black-key groups going *down* ← the keyboard (both keys at once).

Play *piano* (*p*) and use the damper pedal.

2. Using RH 2 3, begin at the middle of the keyboard and play all the 2-black-key groups going *up* → the keyboard (both keys at once).

Play *mezzo forte* (*mf*) and use the damper pedal.

RH

Playing 3-Black-Key Groups

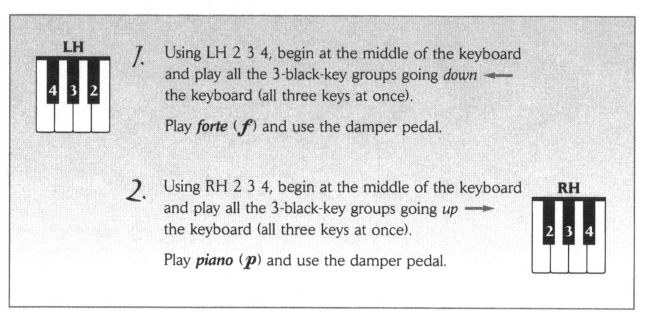

LH

1. Using LH 2 3 4, begin at the middle of the keyboard and play all the 3-black-key groups going *down* ← the keyboard (all three keys at once).

Play *forte* (*f*) and use the damper pedal.

2. Using RH 2 3 4, begin at the middle of the keyboard and play all the 3-black-key groups going *up* → the keyboard (all three keys at once).

Play *piano* (*p*) and use the damper pedal.

RH

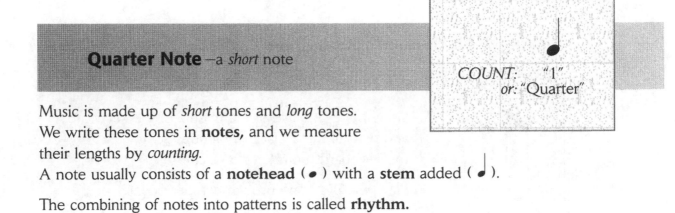

Quarter Note —a *short* note

COUNT: "1"
or: "Quarter"

Music is made up of *short* tones and *long* tones.
We write these tones in **notes,** and we measure
their lengths by *counting.*
A note usually consists of a **notehead** (•) with a **stem** added (♩).

The combining of notes into patterns is called **rhythm.**

Rhythm Exercise: Away from the Keyboard

Clap (or tap) the following rhythm. Clap *once* for each note, counting aloud.
Notice how the **bar lines** divide the music into **measures** of equal duration.

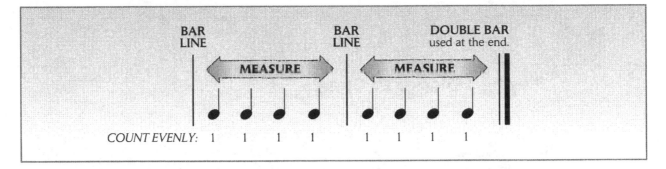

BAR LINE   BAR LINE   DOUBLE BAR used at the end.

← MEASURE →   ← MEASURE →

COUNT EVENLY: 1 1 1 1   1 1 1 1

Technic Exercise: Warm-Ups on 2-Black-Key Groups

Play the following warm-ups one key at a time on 2 black keys in the middle of the
keyboard. Count aloud the first time; say the finger numbers the second time.

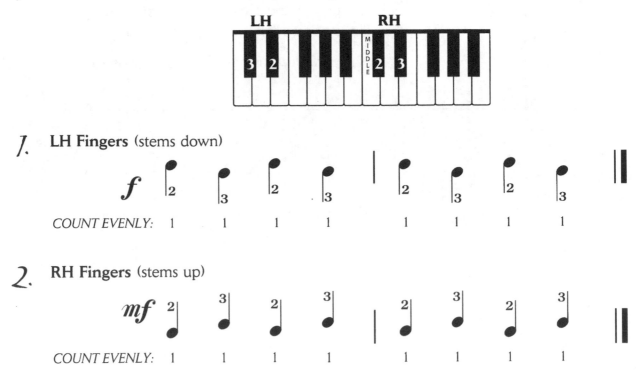

LH   RH

3 2   2 3

1. **LH Fingers** (stems down)

f   2   3   2   3   2   3   2   3

COUNT EVENLY: 1   1   1   1   1   1   1   1

2. **RH Fingers** (stems up)

mf   2   3   2   3   2   3   2   3

COUNT EVENLY: 1   1   1   1   1   1   1   1

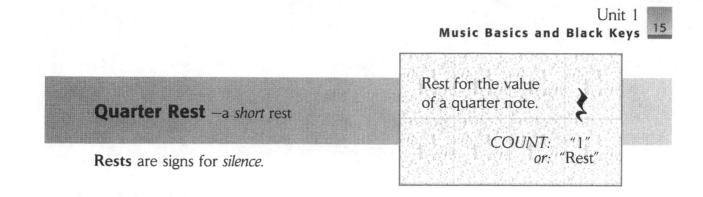

Quarter Rest —a *short* rest

Rest for the value of a quarter note.

COUNT: "1"
or: "Rest"

Rests are signs for *silence*.

Rhythm Exercise: Away from the Keyboard

Clap (or tap) the following rhythm. Clap *once* for each note, counting aloud. Spread (or lift) hands for each rest.

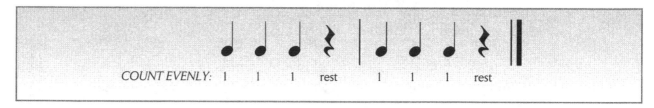

COUNT EVENLY: 1   1   1   rest   1   1   1   rest

Playing 2-Black-Key Groups Going Up and Down

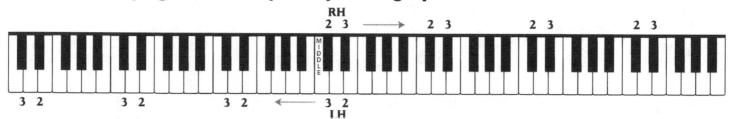

1. With RH 2 3, begin at the middle of the keyboard and play all the 2-black-key groups going *up* the keyboard, using the indicated rhythm and finger numbers (one key at a time).

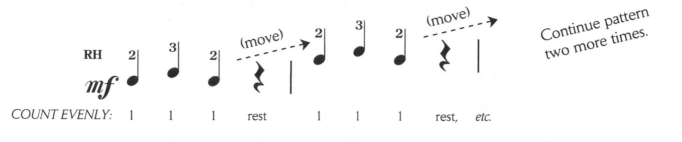

mf

COUNT EVENLY: 1   1   1   rest   1   1   1   rest, *etc.*

2. With LH 2 3, begin at the middle of the keyboard and play all the 2-black-key groups going *down* the keyboard, using the indicated rhythm and finger numbers (one key at a time).

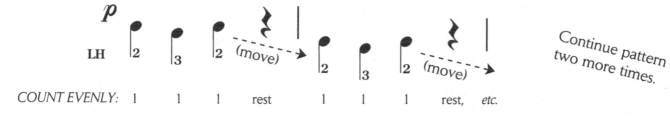

p

COUNT EVENLY: 1   1   1   rest   1   1   1   rest, *etc.*

Half Note—a *longer* note

COUNT: "1 - 2"
or: "Half note"

Rhythm Exercise: Away from the Keyboard

Clap (or tap) the following rhythm.
Clap *once* for each note, counting aloud.

COUNT EVENLY: 1   1   1 – 2   1   1   1 – 2

Technic Exercise: Warm-Ups on 3-Black-Key Groups

Play the following warm-ups one key at a time on 3 black keys in the middle of the keyboard. Count aloud the first time; say the finger numbers the second time.

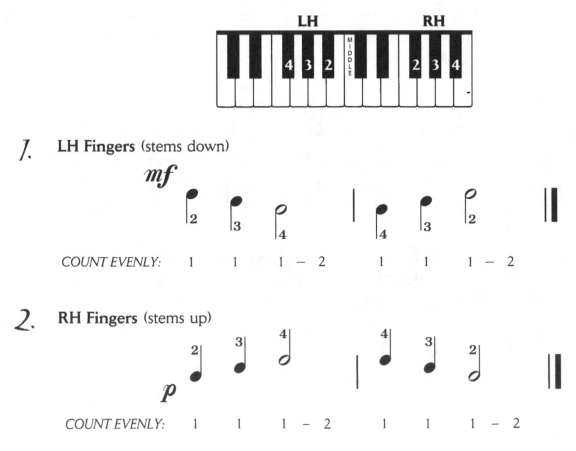

1. **LH Fingers** (stems down)

mf

|2 |3 |4 |4 |3 |2

COUNT EVENLY: 1   1   1 – 2   1   1   1 – 2

2. **RH Fingers** (stems up)

2   3   4   4   3   2

p

COUNT EVENLY: 1   1   1 – 2   1   1   1 – 2

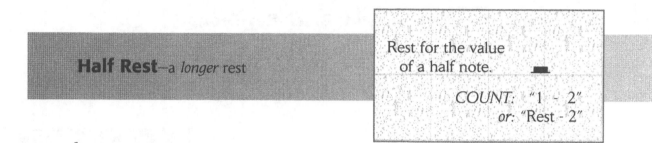

Half Rest—a *longer* rest

Rest for the value
of a half note.

COUNT: "1 - 2"
or: "Rest - 2"

Rhythm Exercise: Away from the Keyboard

Clap (or tap) the following rhythm. Clap *once* for each note, counting aloud.
Spread (or lift) hands for each rest.

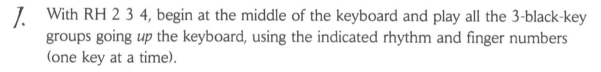

COUNT EVENLY: 1   1   1   1   1 – 2   rest – 2

Playing 3-Black-Key Groups Going Up and Down

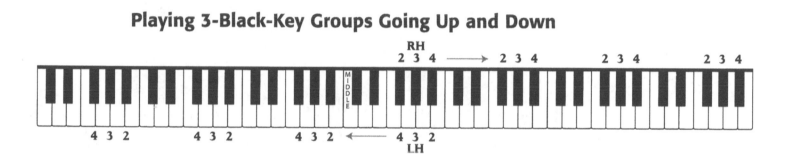

1. With RH 2 3 4, begin at the middle of the keyboard and play all the 3-black-key
groups going *up* the keyboard, using the indicated rhythm and finger numbers
(one key at a time).

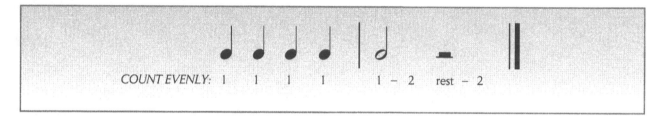

COUNT EVENLY: 1   1   1   1   1 – 2 rest – 2   1   1   1   1   1 – 2 rest – 2 , *etc.*

2. With LH 2 3 4, begin at the middle of the keyboard and play all the 3-black-key
groups going *down* the keyboard, using the indicated rhythm and finger numbers
(one key at a time).

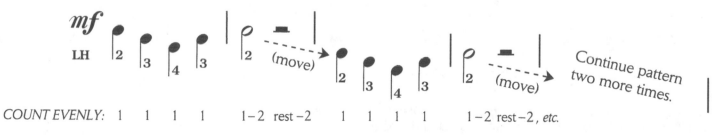

COUNT EVENLY: 1   1   1   1   1 – 2 rest – 2   1   1   1   1   1 – 2 rest – 2, *etc.*

Hands Together on Both Black-Key Groups

1. Clap (or tap) the rhythm evenly, counting aloud.

2. Play & sing (or say) the finger numbers.

3. Play & count.

4. Play & sing the words.

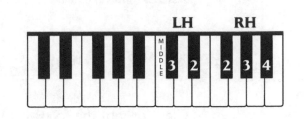

Amazing Grace 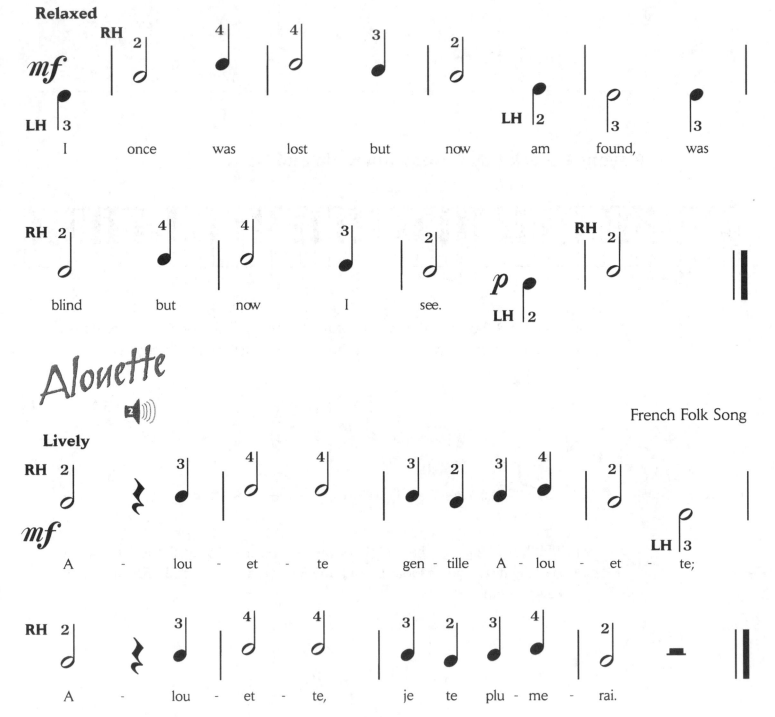 *

John Newton, J. Carroll and D. Clayton

Relaxed

mf

I once was lost but now am found, was

blind but now I see. *p*

Alouette

French Folk Song

Lively

mf

A - lou - et - te gen - tille A - lou - et - te;

A - lou - et - te, je te plu - me - rai.

* This symbol indicates that the selection is on the CD and GM disk recordings.
The number is the "track" number, indicating the order of pieces.

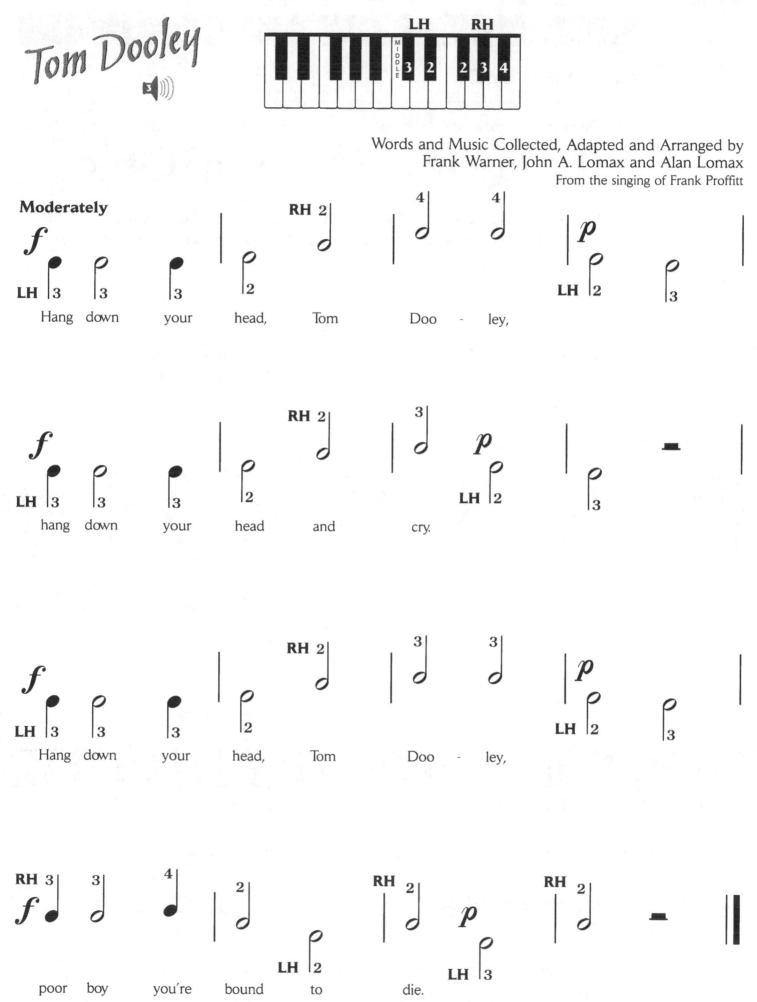

Words and Music Collected, Adapted and Arranged by
Frank Warner, John A. Lomax and Alan Lomax
From the singing of Frank Proffitt

Unit 2

White Keys

Playing White Keys

Piano keys are named for the first
seven letters of the alphabet,
beginning with A:

A B C D E F G

Each white key is recognized by its position in or next to a black-key group.
For example: A's are found between the *upper two keys* of each 3-black-key group.

Play the following, using LH 3 for keys below the middle of the keyboard,
RH 3 for keys above the middle of the keyboard.

Say the name of each key aloud as you play!
Be sure to play *all* the **A**'s on your piano, before going on to the next key.

 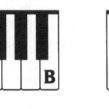 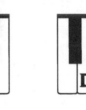

You can now name every white key on your piano!
The key names are **A B C D E F G**, used over and over.

The highest key on your piano is **C**.

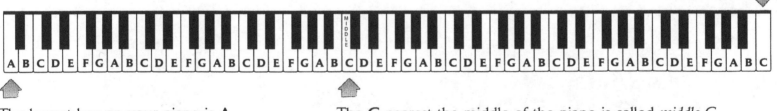

The lowest key on your piano is **A**.   The **C** nearest the middle of the piano is called *middle C*.

Going up the keyboard, the notes sound higher and higher!

Play and name every consecutive white key beginning with bottom **A**.

Use LH 3 for keys below middle **C**, and RH 3 for middle **C** and above.

Written Exercise: Away from the Keyboard

White Keys

1. Write the missing letter names from the music alphabet.

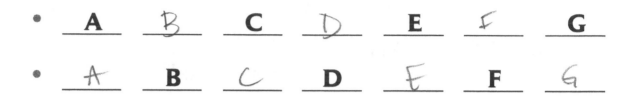

- A B C D E F G
- A B C D E F G

2. On the keyboard below, write the name of every white key going up, beginning with the given **A**.

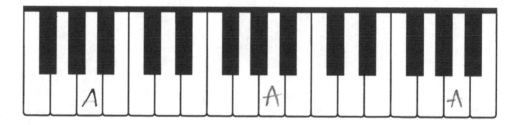

3. Write the letter name on each key marked X.

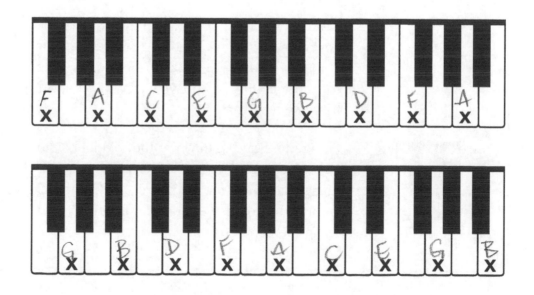

Dotted Half Note—a *long* note

COUNT: "1 - 2 - 3"
or: "Half-note-dot"

Rhythm Exercise: Away from the Keyboard

Clap (or tap) the following rhythm. Clap *once* for each note, counting aloud.
Spread (or lift) hands for each rest.

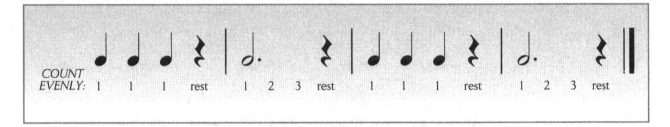

COUNT
EVENLY: 1 1 1 rest 1 2 3 rest 1 1 1 rest 1 2 3 rest

C-D-E Groups

The white keys surrounding the 2-black-key groups are **C-D-E**.

1. Using RH 1 and 3, begin at the middle of the
keyboard and play C and E (both keys at once)
going *up* ⟶ the keyboard. Hold each C and E
for three counts (♩.), playing **piano** (**p**) and using
the damper pedal.

RH 1   3
⟶

2. Using LH 3 and 1, begin at the middle of the
keyboard and play C and E (both keys at once)
going *down* ⟵ the keyboard. Hold each C and
E for three counts (♩.), playing **forte** (**f**) and
using the damper pedal.

LH 3   1
⟵

1. With RH 1 2 3, begin on middle C and play all of the C-D-E groups going *up* the keyboard, using the indicated rhythm and finger numbers.

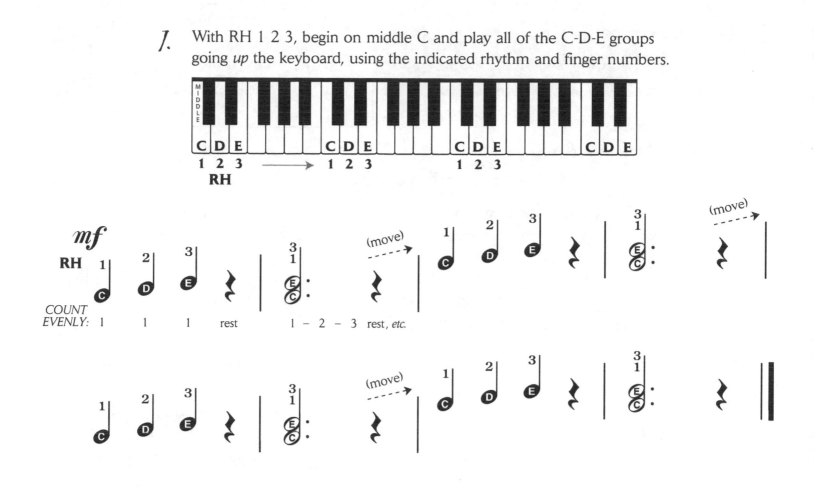

2. With LH 1 2 3, begin on the E above middle C and play all of the C-D-E groups going *down* the keyboard (E-D-C), using the indicated rhythm and finger numbers.

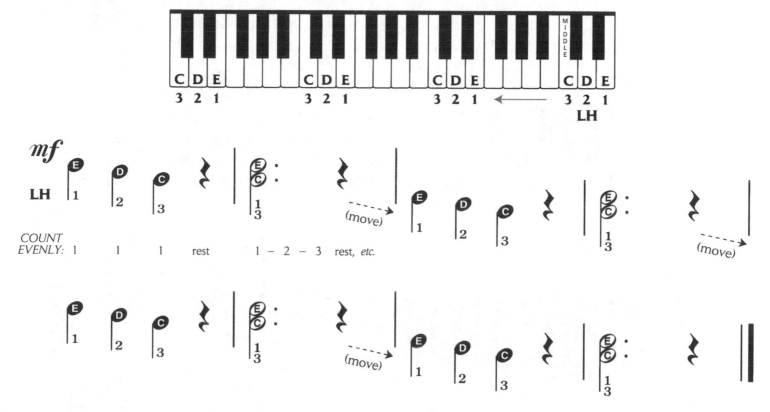

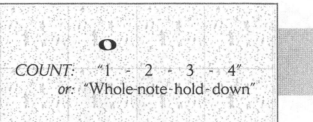

Whole Note—a *very long* note

COUNT: "1 - 2 - 3 - 4"
or: "Whole-note-hold-down"

Rhythm Exercise: Away from the Keyboard

Clap (or tap) the following rhythm. Clap *once* for each note, counting aloud.

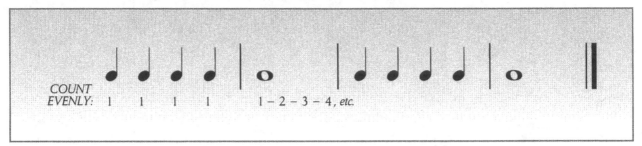

COUNT
EVENLY: 1   1   1   1   1 – 2 – 3 – 4, *etc.*

F-G-A-B Groups

The white keys surrounding the 3-black-key groups are **F-G-A-B.**

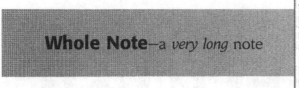

1. Using RH 1 and 3, begin at the middle of the keyboard and play F and A (both keys at once) going *up* the keyboard. Hold each F and A four counts, playing ***mezzo forte*** (**mf**) and using the damper pedal. *Optional:* Repeat No. 1 with RH fingers 2 and 4 on G and B.

RH   1   3

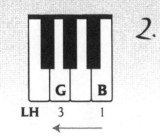

LH   3   1

2. Using LH 3 and 1, begin at the middle of the keyboard and play G and B (both keys at once) going *down* the keyboard. Hold each G and B four counts, playing ***forte*** (**f**) and using the damper pedal. *Optional:* Repeat No. 2 with LH fingers 4 and 2 on F and A.

Whole Rest—a *very long* rest

Rest for the value of a whole note (or one whole measure).

▬

COUNT: "1 - 2 - 3 - 4"
or: "Rest - 2 - 3 - 4"

1. With RH 1 2 3 4, begin on the F above middle C and play all of the F-G-A-B groups going *up* the keyboard, using the indicated rhythm and finger numbers.

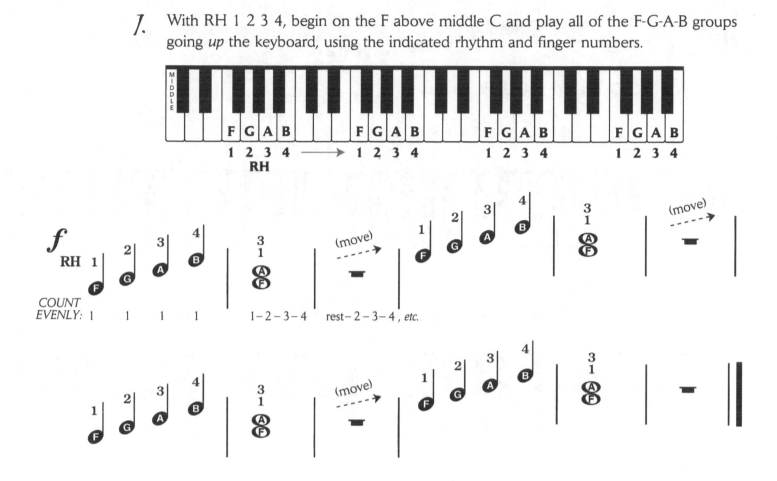

2. With LH 1 2 3 4, begin on the B above middle C and play all of the F-G-A-B groups going *down* the keyboard (B-A-G-F), using the indicated rhythm and finger numbers.

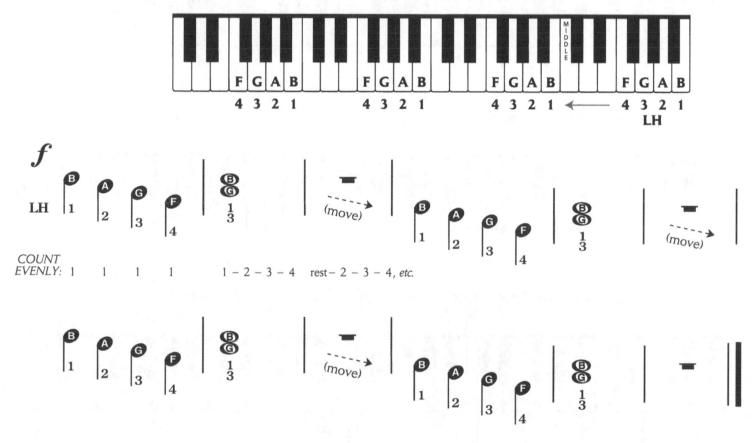

Written Exercise: Away from the Keyboard

C-D-E and F-G-A-B Groups

1. Circle each C-D-E group on the keyboard below.

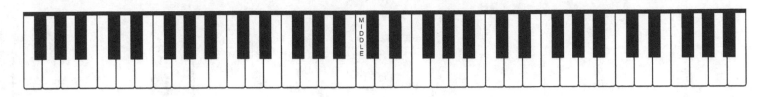

2. Write the letter name on each C, D and E on the keyboard below.

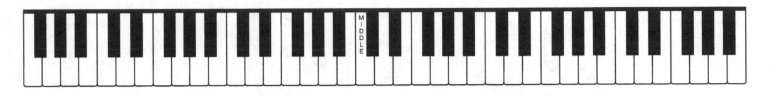

3. Circle each F-G-A-B group on the keyboard below.

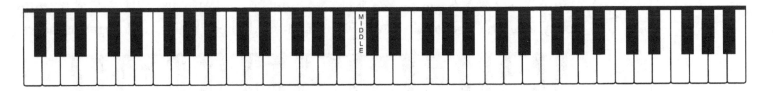

4. Write the letter name on each F and A on the keyboard below.

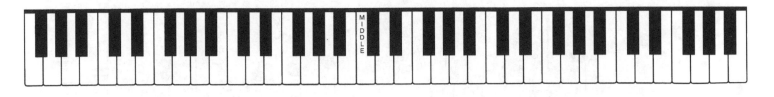

5. Write the letter name on each G and B on the keyboard below.

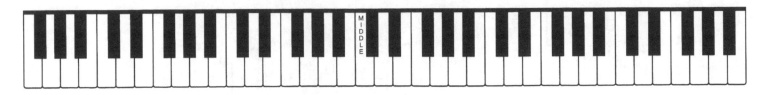

Time Signature

Music has numbers at the beginning called the **time signature**.
The top number tells the number of **beats** (counts) in each measure.
The bottom number tells the kind of note that gets *one* beat (count).

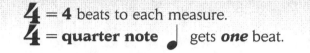

4 = **4** beats to each measure.
4 = **quarter note** ♩ gets *one* beat.

	Note	Rest	Count	Total number of counts in $\frac{4}{4}$
QUARTER	♩	𝄽	"1"	1
HALF	♩	▬	"1 - 2"	2
DOTTED HALF	♩.	▬ + 𝄽	"1 - 2 - 3"	3
WHOLE	o	▬	"1 - 2 - 3 - 4"	4

Rhythm Exercise: Away from the Keyboard

Clap (or tap) the following rhythms, counting aloud.

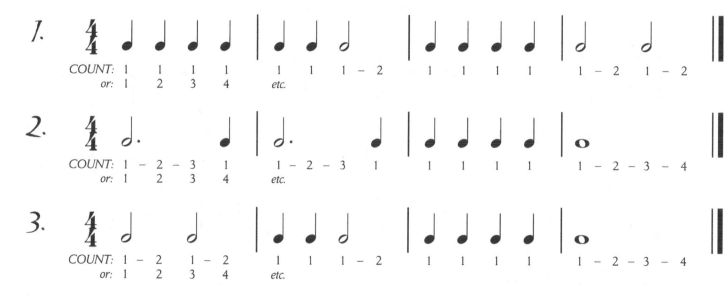

1.
COUNT: 1 1 1 1   1 1 1 – 2   1 1 1 1   1 – 2   1 – 2
or: 1 2 3 4   *etc.*

2.
COUNT: 1 – 2 – 3 1   1 – 2 – 3 1   1 1 1 1   1 – 2 – 3 – 4
or: 1 2 3 4   *etc.*

3.
COUNT: 1 – 2   1 – 2   1 1 1 – 2   1 1 1 1   1 – 2 – 3 – 4
or: 1 2 3 4   *etc.*

Left Hand C Position

Place the LH on the keyboard so that the *5th finger* falls on the *C below middle C.* Let the remaining fingers fall naturally on the next 4 white keys. Keep the fingers curved and relaxed.

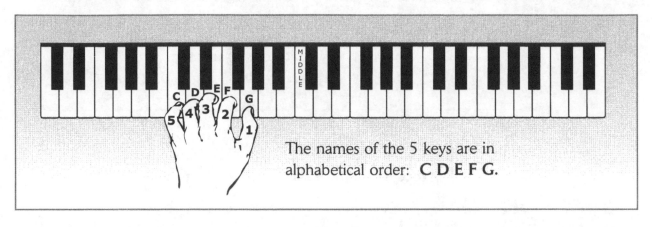

The names of the 5 keys are in alphabetical order: **C D E F G.**

Technic Exercise: Left Hand Warm-Ups

Play the following warm-ups using a steady beat and a curved hand position. Say the name of each note aloud as you play. Repeat until you can play smoothly and evenly.

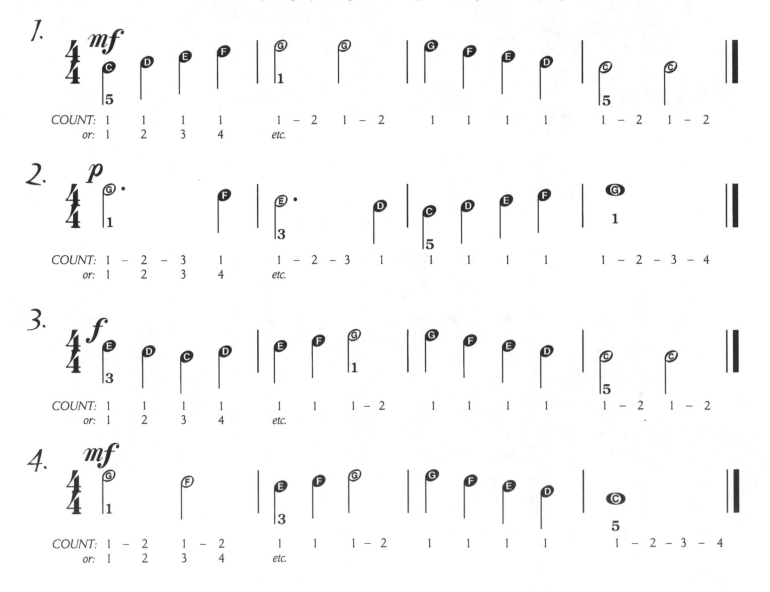

Right Hand C Position

Place the RH on the keyboard so that the *1st finger* falls on *middle C*. Let the remaining fingers fall naturally on the next 4 white keys. Keep the fingers curved and relaxed.

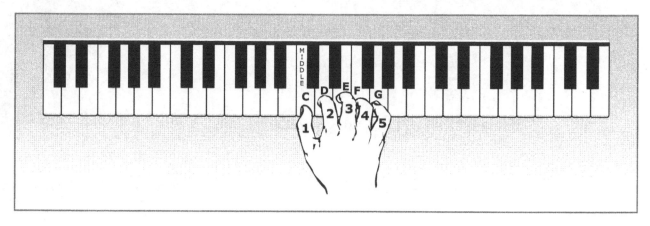

Technic Exercise: Right Hand Warm-Ups

Play the following warm-ups using a steady beat and a curved hand position. Say the name of each note aloud as you play. Repeat until you can play smoothly and evenly.

Optional: Play the warm-ups on pages 28 and 29 hands together.

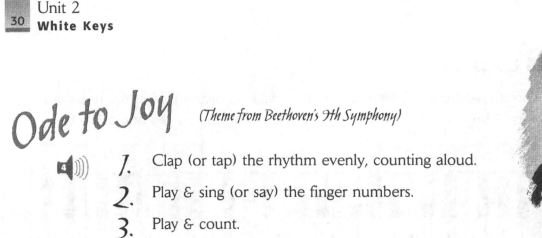

Ode to Joy *(Theme from Beethoven's 9th Symphony)*

1. Clap (or tap) the rhythm evenly, counting aloud.

2. Play & sing (or say) the finger numbers.

3. Play & count.

4. Play & sing (or say) the note names.

> Beethoven was already beginning to lose
> his hearing when he wrote his great
> 9th Symphony. In the final movement,
> a chorus sings this famous melody.

RH C Position (see page 29)

Ludwig van Beethoven
(1770–1827)

Joyfully

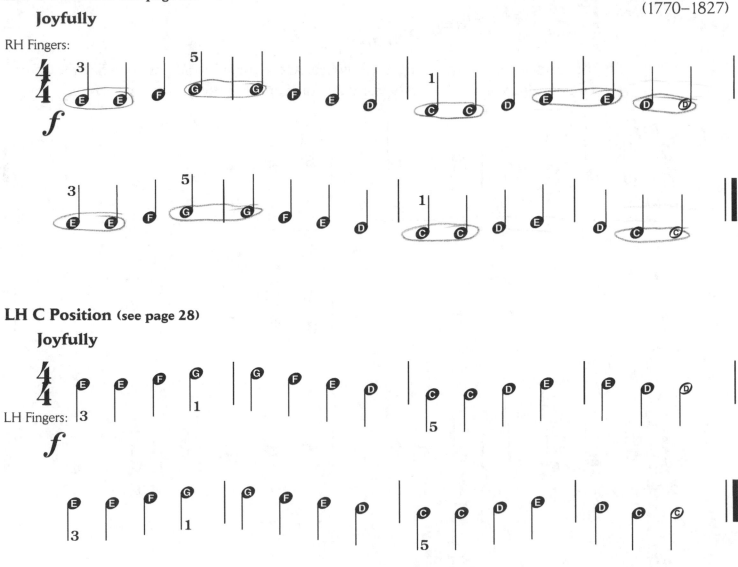

LH C Position (see page 28)

Joyfully

Optional: After playing hands separately, play *Ode to Joy* hands together.

Aura Lee

Elvis Presley, c. 1956. Archive Photos, New York.

1. Clap (or tap) the rhythm evenly, counting aloud.

2. Play & sing (or say) the finger numbers.

3. Play & count.

4. Play & sing (or say) the note names.

This folk melody was made into a popular song, "Love Me Tender," sung by Elvis Presley.

RH C Position

Moderately

LH C Position

Moderately

Optional: After playing hands separately, play *Aura Lee* hands together.

Unit 3

The Staff

In Units 1 and 2, you played music from letter notes. Most music, however, is written on a **staff** of 5 lines and 4 spaces.

The **Treble Clef Sign** helps identify notes *above* middle C.

Written Exercise: Away from the Keyboard

1. Trace these treble clef signs.

Start Here   End Here

2. Draw four treble clef signs.

The **Bass Clef Sign** helps identify notes *below* middle C.

Written Exercise: Away from the Keyboard

3. Trace these bass clef signs.
The two dots are in the top 2 spaces.

Start Here

Make the 2 dots last.

4. Draw four bass clef signs.

Line Notes and Space Notes

Some notes are written on lines and some are written in spaces.

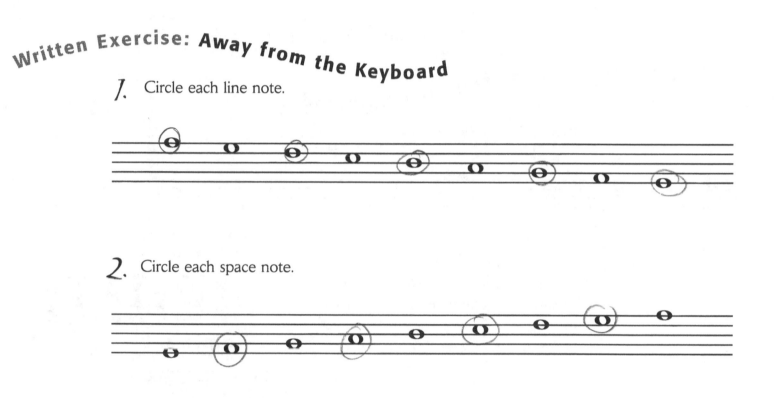

Written Exercise: Away from the Keyboard

1. Circle each line note.

2. Circle each space note.

3. Write the indicated note on the given line or space. Write the notehead first. Turn stems
   up for notes *on* or *below* the third line; turn stems down for notes *above* the third line.

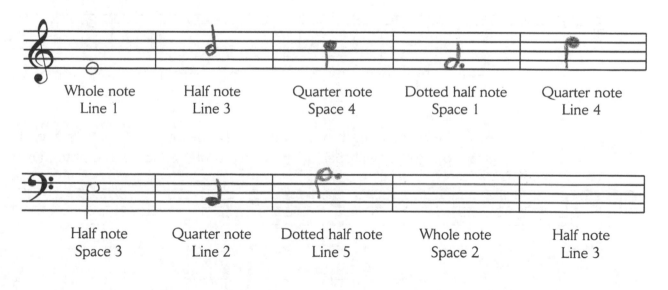

| Whole note | Half note | Quarter note | Dotted half note | Quarter note |
| Line 1 | Line 3 | Space 4 | Space 1 | Line 4 |

| Half note | Quarter note | Dotted half note | Whole note | Half note |
| Space 3 | Line 2 | Line 5 | Space 2 | Line 3 |

The Bass Clef

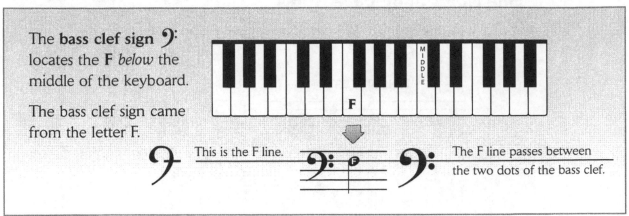

The **bass clef sign** 𝄢 locates the **F** *below* the middle of the keyboard.

The bass clef sign came from the letter F.

This is the F line.   The F line passes between the two dots of the bass clef.

Bass notes are usually played with the left hand.

Written Exercise: Away from the Keyboard

Circle each F in the bass clef.

By moving up or down from the F line, you can name any note on the bass staff.

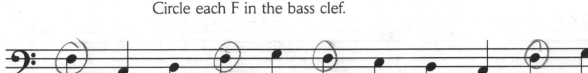

Write and Play Exercise

1. Write the name of each note in the square below it—then play and say the note names.

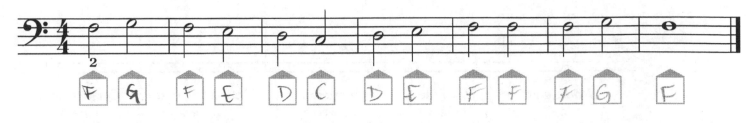

F G   F E   D C   D E   F F   F G   F

2. Write the name of each note in the square below it. The letters in each group of squares will spell a familiar word. Play and say the note names.

F E E   E D G E   F E E D   E G G   E D

The Treble Clef

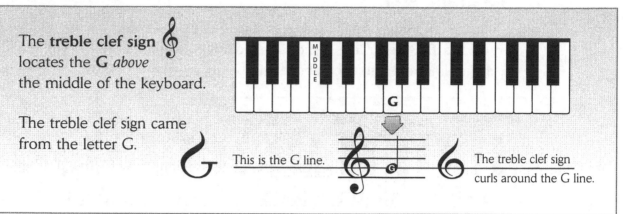

The **treble clef sign** locates the **G** *above* the middle of the keyboard.

The treble clef sign came from the letter G.

This is the G line.

The treble clef sign curls around the G line.

Treble notes are usually played with the right hand.

Written Exercise: Away from the Keyboard

Circle each G in the treble clef.

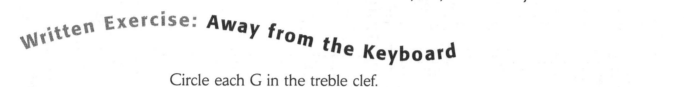

By moving up or down from the G line, you can name any note on the treble staff.

A short line called a **leger line** is added below the staff to identify middle C.

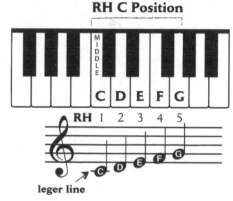

RH C Position

C D E F G

RH 1 2 3 4 5

leger line

Write and Play Exercise

1. Write the name of each note in the square below it—then play and say the note names.

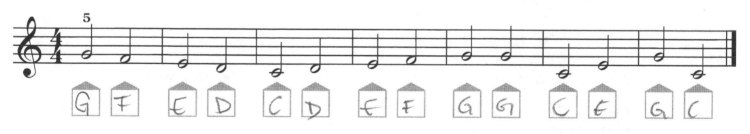

G F E D C D E F G G C E G C

2. Write the name of each note in the square below it. The letters in each group of squares will spell a familiar word. Play and say the note names.

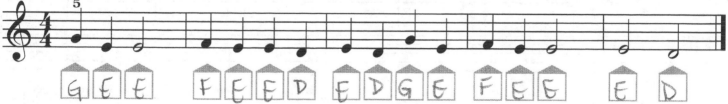

G E E F E E D E D G E F E E E D

The Grand Staff

When the bass staff and the treble staff are joined together by a brace, they make the **Grand Staff.** A leger line, a short line added between the two staves, identifies middle C. Leger lines are also used above and below the grand staff to extend its range.

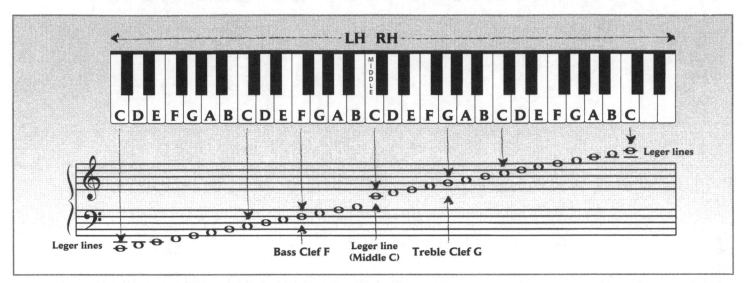

C Position on the Grand Staff

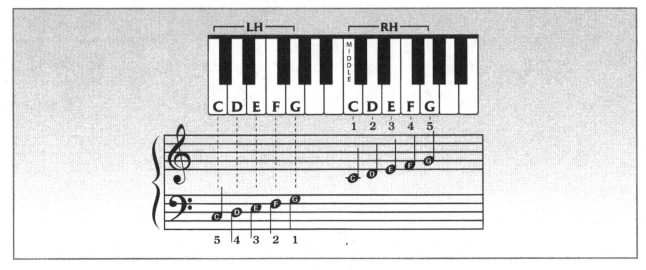

Write and Play Exercise

Write the name of each note in the square below it—then play and say the note names.

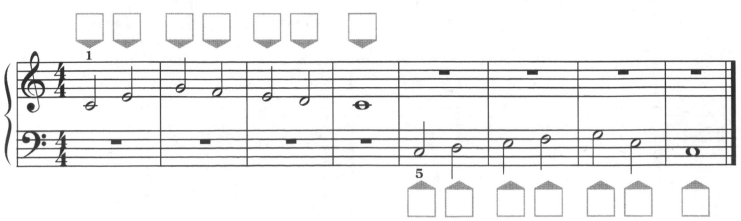

Written Exercise: Away from the Keyboard

1. In each box write the number of counts the note or rest receives in 4/4 time. Review page 27.

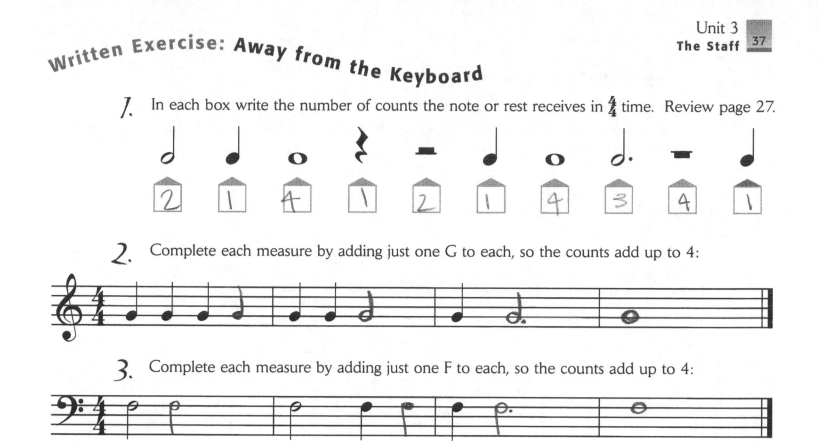

| 2 | 1 | 4 | 1 | 2 | 1 | 4 | 3 | 4 | 1 |

2. Complete each measure by adding just one G to each, so the counts add up to 4:

3. Complete each measure by adding just one F to each, so the counts add up to 4:

Write and Play Exercise

1. Add *bar lines* below (like the first one shown), to divide the music into measures of 4 counts each.

2. Add a *whole rest* in each measure to indicate silence for the LH or RH.

3. Write the name of each note in the box above it.

Lightly Row

Moderately

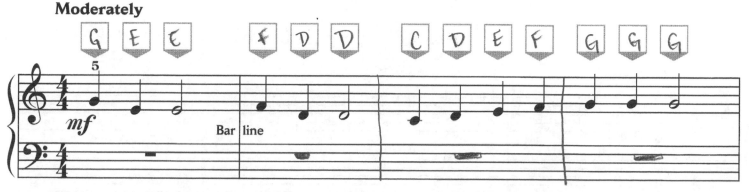

G E E   F D D   C D E F   G G G

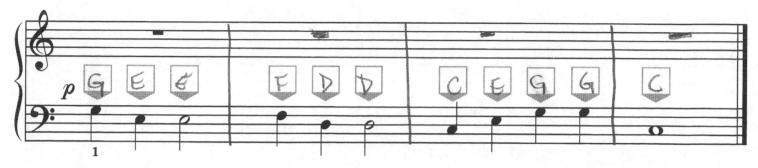

G E E   F D D   C E G G   C

Sight Reading Made Easy—Part 1

Locate the starting note. If the next note is on the *same* line or space of the staff, play the *same* key again. If the note moves *up* on the staff, play a higher key. If the note moves *down* on the staff, play a lower key.

Practice Exercise: Sight Reading

Every musician must learn to read and play at sight (the first time the music is performed). Follow the practice directions, working to play each example perfectly the first time.

1. Clap (or tap) & count.   *2.* Play & count.   *3.* Play & sing (or say) the note names.

Sight Reading Made Easy—Part 2

Skipping Along

In addition to stepping up or down on the keyboard and staff, notes may also skip in either direction.

Note-reading is very easy if you remember that the notes on the staff are like a picture of the way the fingers move on the keys.

Notes skipping *up* from space to *next* space, or line to *next* line: *skip* one white key.

Notes skipping *down* from space to *next* space, or line to *next* line: *skip* one white key.

The Repeat Sign means *repeat from the beginning.*

Mexican Hat Dance

With energy

mf

1. Play it! Play it! Play the fa - mous hat dance!
2. Dance it! Dance it! Dance the fa - mous hat dance!

Play it! Play it! Play it now for me!
Dance it! Dance it! It's such fun to see!

Repeat sign

Now go back and play Lightly Row on page 37. This piece uses steps, skips and repeated notes.

Unit 4

Melodic and Harmonic Intervals

Melodic Intervals

Distances between tones are measured in **intervals,** called 2nds, 3rds, 4ths, 5ths, etc. Notes played *separately* make a **melody.** We call the intervals between these notes **melodic intervals.**

Play these melodic 2nds & 3rds. Listen to the sound of each interval.

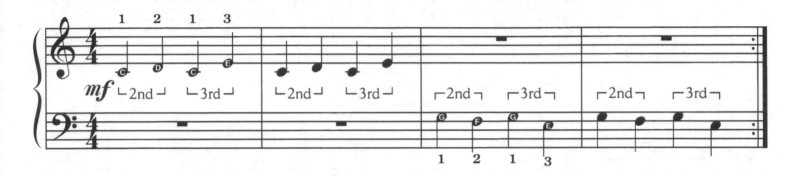

2nds

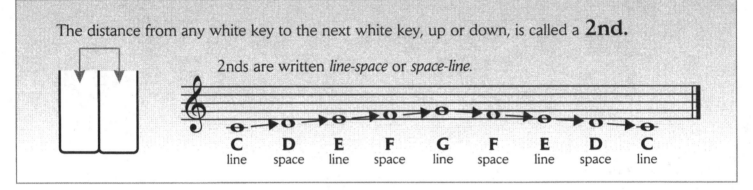

The distance from any white key to the next white key, up or down, is called a **2nd.**

2nds are written *line-space* or *space-line.*

C D E F G F E D C
line space line space line space line space line

Seconds

Moderately fast

C Name the note.

The following practice procedure is recommended for the rest of the pieces in this book:

1. Clap (or tap) the rhythm evenly, counting aloud.
2. Play & count.
3. Play & sing (or say) the note names.

mf Line-space, space-line, next-door neigh-bors, Space-line, line-space, These are sec-onds!

G Name the note.

3rds

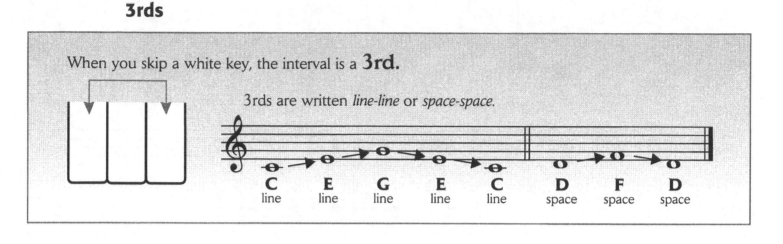

When you skip a white key, the interval is a **3rd.**

3rds are written *line-line* or *space-space.*

C	E	G	E	C	D	F	D
line	line	line	line	line	space	space	space

Thirds

Moderately slow

Name the note.

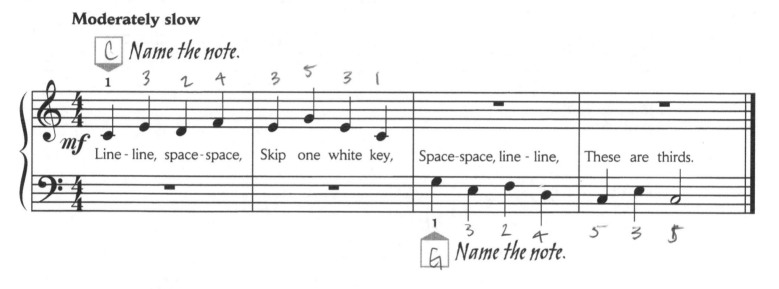

Line - line, space - space, Skip one white key, Space-space, line - line, These are thirds.

Name the note.

Au Claire de la Lune

Moderately

Name the note.

Tisket, a Tasket

Moderately fast

5

Name the note.

Name the note.

Practice Exercise: Sight Reading

Write and Play Exercise

Interval Reading

1. Write the interval name (2nd or 3rd) on the line below the staff. Then play, using the correct fingers.

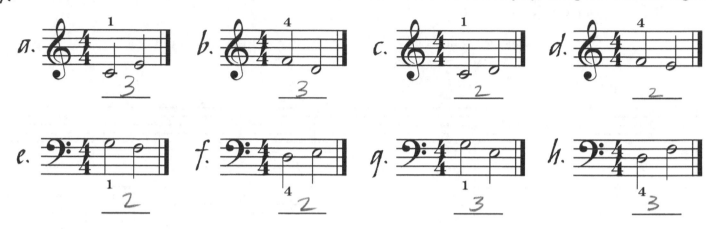

2nds

2. Write a half note *up* a 2nd from the given note in the first four measures of each line below. Turn all the stems in the treble clef *up*. Turn all the stems in the bass clef *down*.

3. Write the name of each note in the square below it—then play and say the note names.

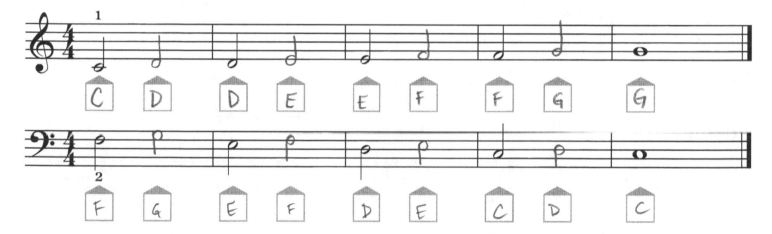

3rds

4. Write a half note *up* a 3rd from the given note in the first four measures of each line below. Turn all the stems in the treble clef *up*. Turn all the stems in the bass clef *down*.

5. Write the name of each note in the square below it—then play and say the note names.

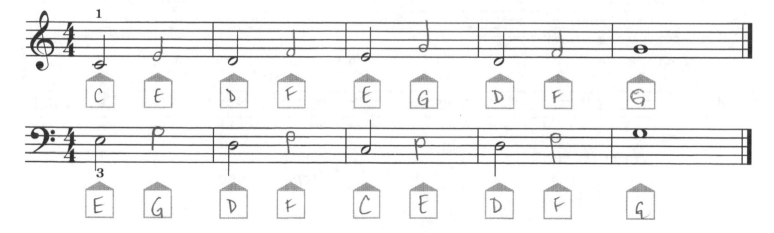

Harmonic Intervals

Notes played *together* make **harmony.** We call the intervals between these notes **harmonic intervals.**

Play these harmonic 2nds & 3rds. Listen to the sound of each interval.

Rockin' Intervals

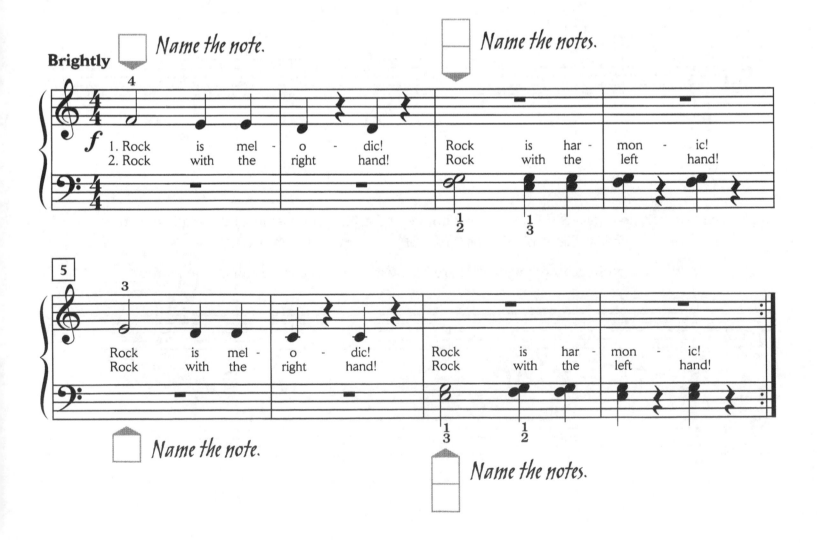

More Harmonic 2nds and 3rds

Play the harmonic 2nds & 3rds. Say the name of each interval as you play.

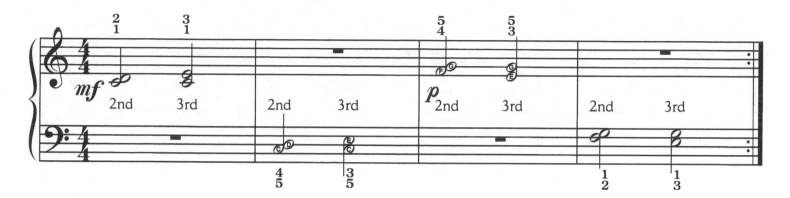

Harmonica Rock

1. Write the name of each harmonic interval (2nd or 3rd) in the box above it.

2. Play, saying the name of each interval.

Steady rock tempo

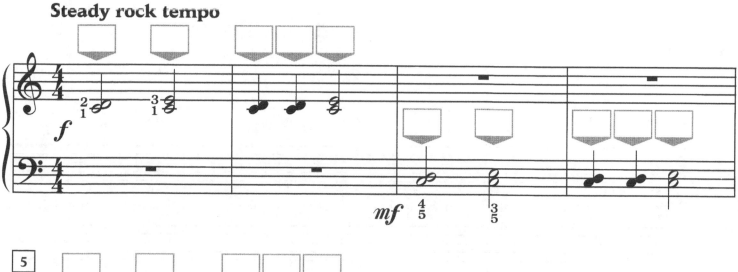

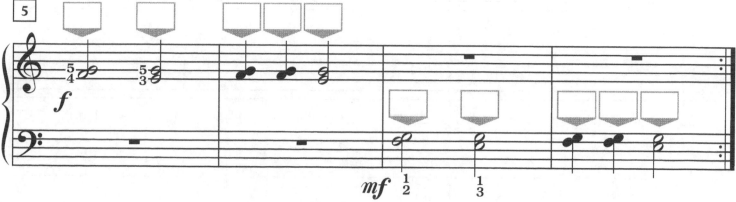

Melodic 4ths and 5ths

Play these melodic 4ths & 5ths. Listen to the sound of each interval.

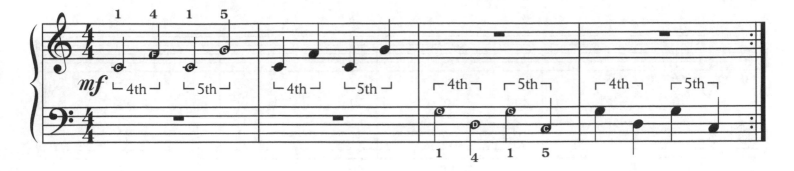

4ths

When you skip 2 white keys, the interval is a **4th.**

4ths are written *line-space* or *space-line*.

| C | F | D | G | | C | F | D | G |
| space | line | line | space | | line | space | space | line |

Fourths

Moderately slow

Line to space, skip two white keys; Space to line, skip two white keys;

Space to line; line to space, That's the way to play a fourth!

5ths

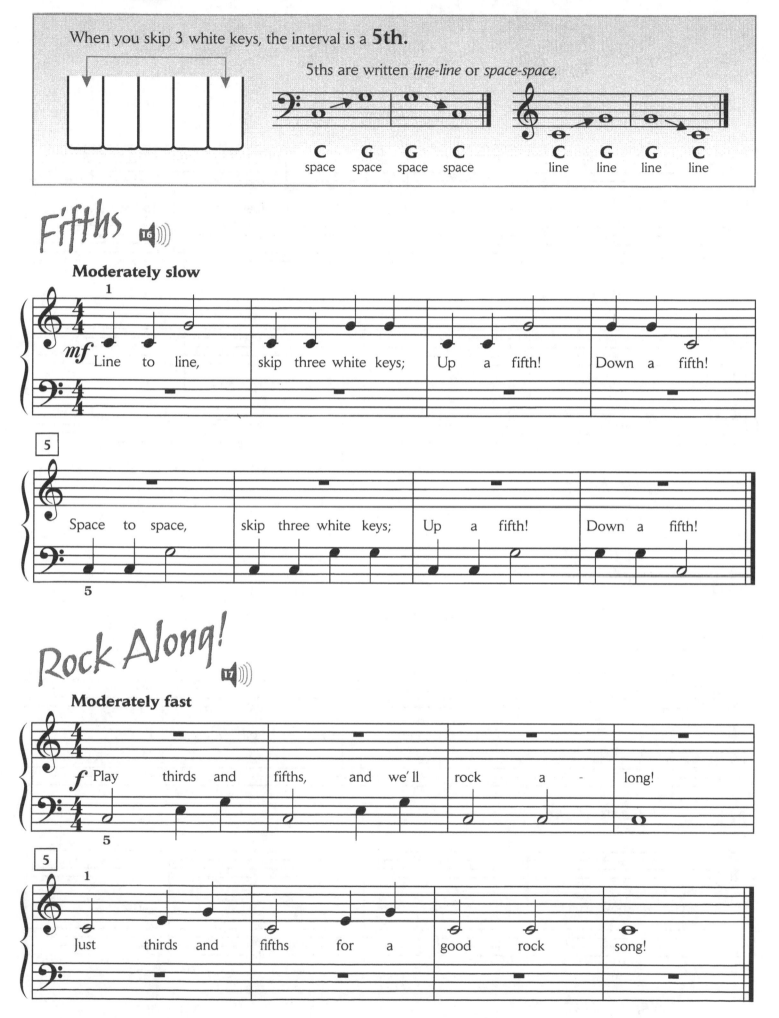

When you skip 3 white keys, the interval is a **5th.**

5ths are written *line-line* or *space-space.*

C	G	G	C
space	space	space	space

C	G	G	C
line	line	line	line

Fifths 16

Moderately slow

mf Line to line, | skip three white keys; | Up a fifth! | Down a fifth!

Space to space, | skip three white keys; | Up a fifth! | Down a fifth!

Rock Along! 17

Moderately fast

f Play thirds and | fifths, and we'll | rock a - | long!

Just thirds and | fifths for a | good rock | song!

Good King Wenceslas

Find and circle the 4ths before you play!

Moderately fast

f Good King Wen - ces - las look'd out, On the feast of Ste - phen,

Name the note.

When the snow lay round a - bout, Deep and crisp and e - ven.

Name the note.

My Fifth

Find and circle the 5ths before you play!

Seriously

p This is my fifth, and may - be you've heard;

Name the note.

Beet - hov - en's fifth is *f* on - ly a third!

Name the note.

Write and Play Exercise

Interval Reading

1. Write the interval name (4th or 5th) on the line below the staff. Then play, using the correct fingers.

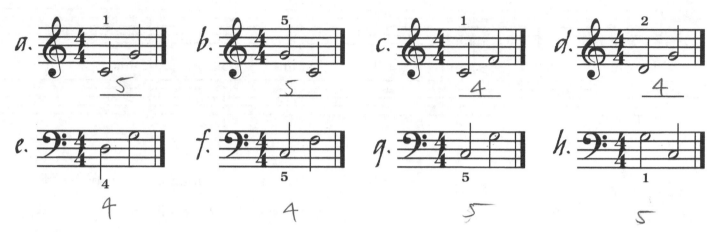

4ths

2. Write a half note *up* a 4th from the given note in each measure below.
Turn all the stems in the treble clef *up*. Turn all the stems in the bass clef *down*.

3. Write the name of each note in the square below it—then play and say the note names.

4. Write a half note *down* a 4th from the given note in each measure below.
Turn all the stems in the treble clef *up*. Turn the stems of D, E, F and G in the bass clef *down*.
Turn the stem of the C in the bass clef *up*.

5. Write the name of each note in the square below it—then play and say the note names.

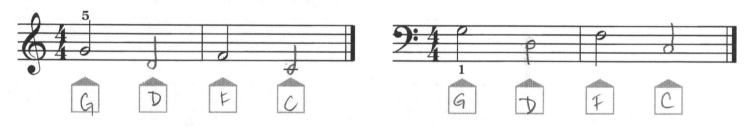

5ths

6. Write a half note *up* a 5th from each C and *down* a 5th from each G on each staff below.
Turn all the stems in the treble clef *up*. Turn the stem of the G in the bass clef *down*.
Turn the stem of the C in the bass clef *up*.

7. Write the name of each note in the square below it—then play and say the note names.

Harmonic 4ths and 5ths

Play these harmonic 4ths & 5ths. Listen to the sound of each interval.

Jingle Bells

1. Find one *melodic* 4th & one *melodic* 5th in the RH.

2. Find all the *harmonic* 4ths & 5ths in the LH.

3. Play the RH & LH separately at first, then together.

Name the note.

Name the notes.

Merrily

f Jin - gle, bells!   Jin - gle, bells!   Jin - gle   all   the   way!

Oh, what fun it   is to ride a   one - horse o - pen   sleigh!

Jin - gle, bells!   Jin - gle, bells!   Jin - gle all the   way!

Oh, what fun it   is to ride a   one - horse o - pen   sleigh!

5. These notes are in SPACES. Write the name of each note in the box below it.

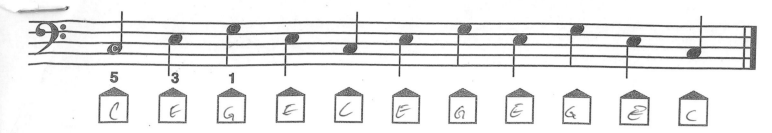

5   3   1

| C | E | G | E | C | E | G | E | G | e | C |

6. These notes are on LINES. Write the name of each note in the box below.

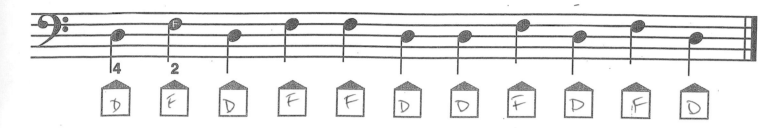

4   2

| D | F | D | F | F | D | D | F | D | F | D |

7. Here are notes on LINES & SPACES. Write the name of each note in the box.

5

| C | E | D | F | E | G | E | F | D | E | C |

1

| G | E | F | D | E | C | E | D | F | E | G |

8. Each of these notes repeats on the SAME line or space.
Write the name of each note in the box below it.

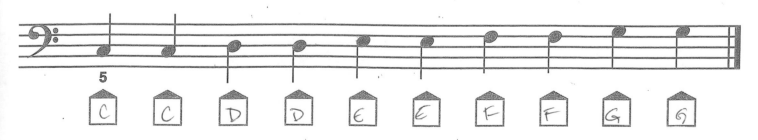

5

| C | C | D | D | E | E | F | F | G | G |

9. Below each note on this page, write the finger number used to play it in LH C POSITION.

10. Play all the notes on this page in LH C POSITION.

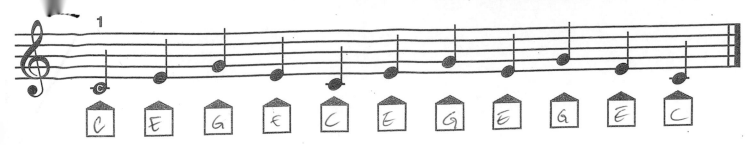

C	E	G	E	C	E	G	E	G	E	C

6. These notes are in SPACES. Write the name of each note in the box below.

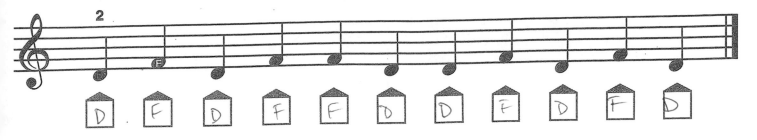

D	F	D	F	F	D	D	F	D	F	D

7. Here are notes on LINES & SPACES. Write the name of each note in the box.

C	E	D	F	E	G	E	F	D	E	C

G	E	F	D	E	C	E	D	F	E	G

8. When a note repeats on the SAME line or space, the note is repeated on the keyboard. Write the name of each note in the box below it.

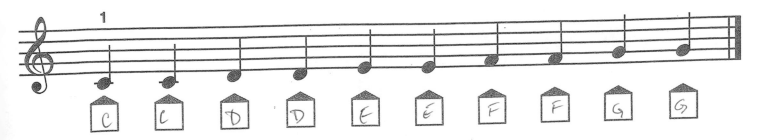

C	C	D	D	E	E	F	F	G	G

9. Above each note on this page, write the finger number used to play it in RH C POSITION.

10. Play all the notes on this page in RH C POSITION.

Use after page 17.

SONATINA IN C

Brightly

Slower

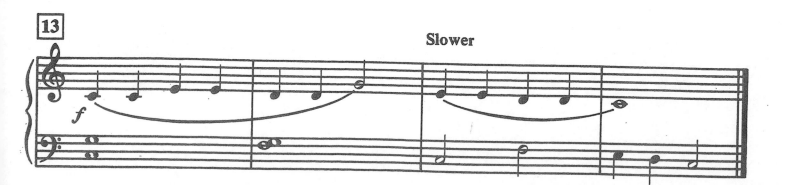

More Harmonic 4ths and 5ths

Play these harmonic 4ths & 5ths. Say the name of each interval as you play.

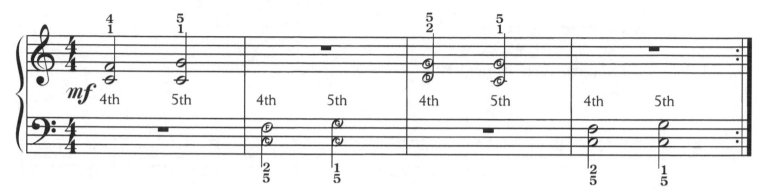

Dueling Harmonics

1. Write the name of each harmonic interval in the box above it.

2. Play, saying the name of each interval.

Moderately

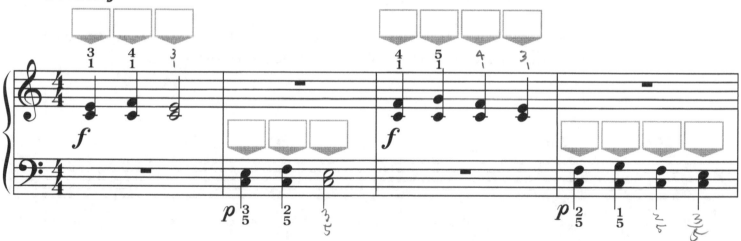

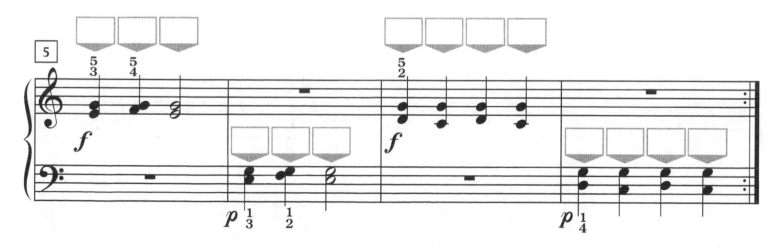

Written Exercise: Away from the Keyboard

Harmonic Intervals

1. Circle each harmonic 4th.

2. Write a whole note *above* the given note in each measure below to make the indicated harmonic interval.

3. Write the names of the notes in the squares. Write the name of the lower note in the lower square; the name of the higher note in the higher square.

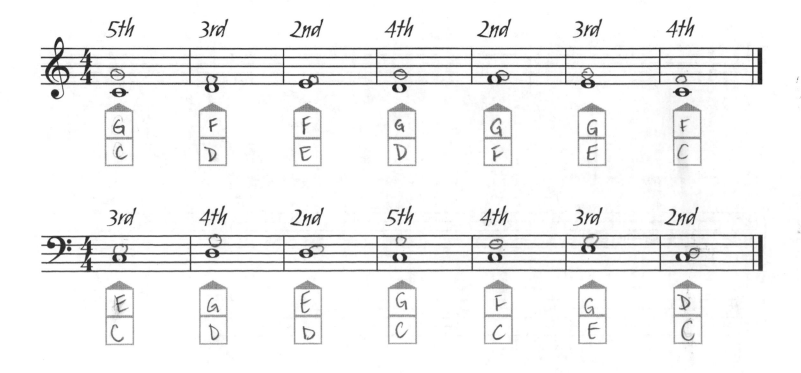

Interval Review

Melodies

22))) This piece reviews melodic 2nds, 3rds, 4ths & 5ths.
Name all the melodic intervals in this piece before you play it.

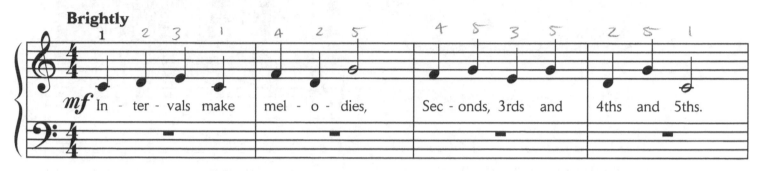

Harmonies

23))) This piece reviews harmonic 2nds, 3rds, 4ths & 5ths.
Name all the harmonic intervals in this piece before you play it.

Unit 5

Middle C Position

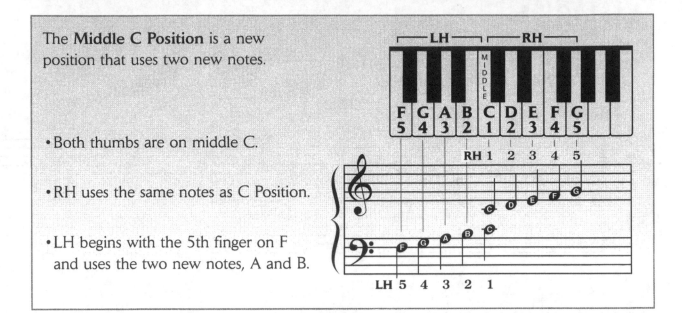

The **Middle C Position** is a new position that uses two new notes.

- Both thumbs are on middle C.

- RH uses the same notes as C Position.

- LH begins with the 5th finger on F and uses the two new notes, A and B.

Play and say the note names. Do this several times!

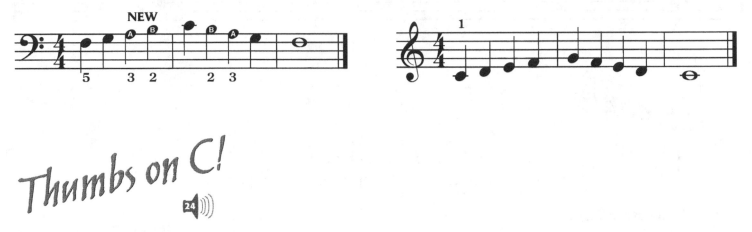

Thumbs on C!

24

Moderately slow

Camptown Races

Stephen Foster composed over 200 songs. He was one of the first Americans to support himself as a full-time composer of songs.

Stephen Foster
(1826–1864)

Lively

Camp-town la-dies sing this song, doo-dah, doo-dah.

Camp-town race-track five miles long, oh, doo-dah day.

New Dynamic Signs

crescendo (gradually louder)

diminuendo (gradually softer)

Theme from Surprise Symphony

Haydn was known as the "Father of the Symphony." Although he wasn't the first composer to write them, he made symphonies longer and for larger orchestras.

Franz Joseph Haydn
(1732–1809)

Moderately

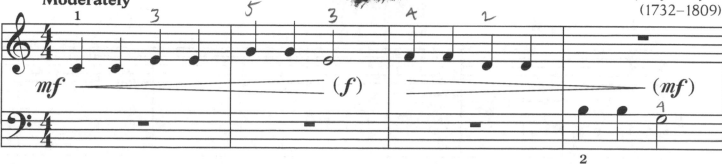

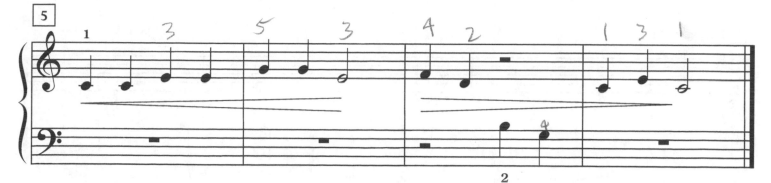

Practice Exercise: Sight Reading

Moderately slow

Written Exercise: Away from the Keyboard

1. Write the name of each note in the square below it—then play and say the note names.

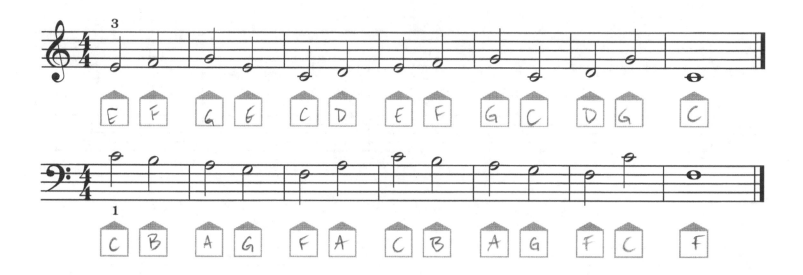

E F G E C D E F G C D G C

C B A G F A C B A G F C F

2. Connect the dots on the matching boxes.

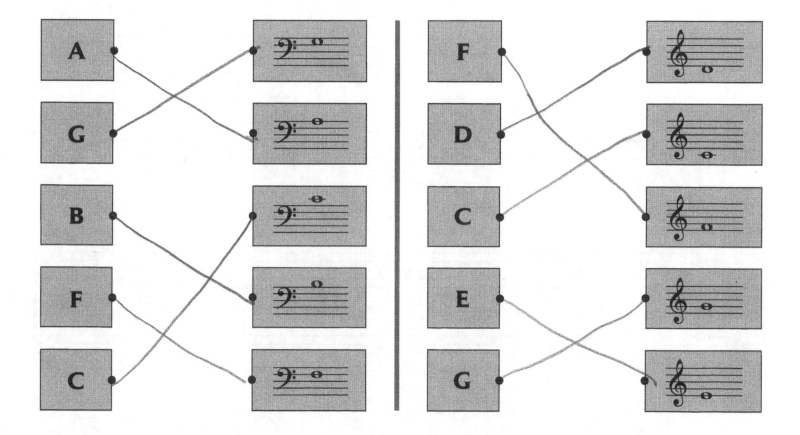

Jolly Old Saint Nicholas

Traditional

Happily

Theme from
Eine Kleine Nachtmusik*

> Mozart was a famous child prodigy who began studying the piano at age four with his father. He composed music for all mediums. This famous theme was originally written for strings and has remained popular from Mozart's time to the present.

Wolfgang Amadeus Mozart
(1756–1791)

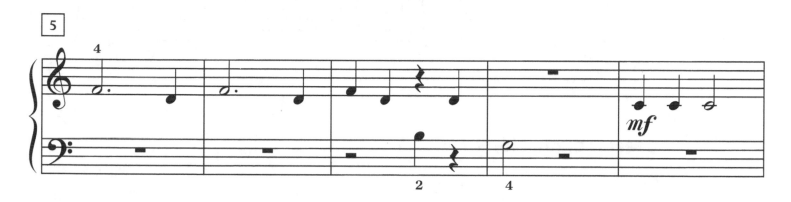

*A Little Night Music

Unit 6

Chords

A **chord** is three or more notes played together.

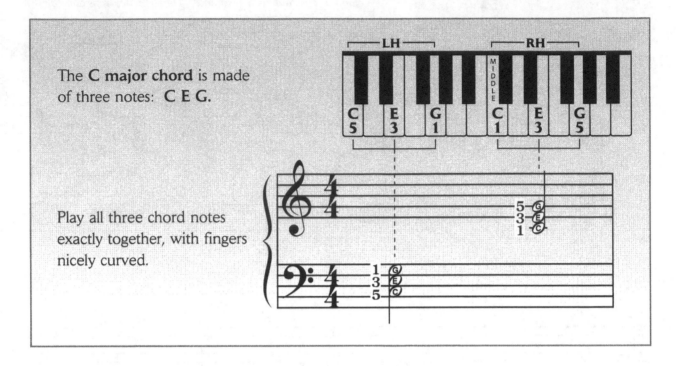

The **C major chord** is made of three notes: **C E G.**

Play all three chord notes exactly together, with fingers nicely curved.

C Major Chords for RH

Play and count.

C Major Chords for LH

Play and count.

Optional: Play the above examples hands together.

Written Exercise: Away from the Keyboard

1. In the squares above the staff, write the names of the notes in each C major chord.

2. Circle each C major chord.

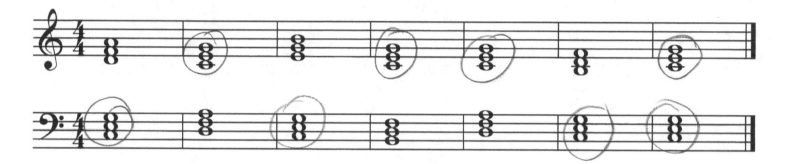

Interval Review

3. Write a half note *up* from the given note in each measure below to make the indicated melodic interval. Turn all the stems in the treble clef *up*. Turn all the stems in the bass clef *down*.

4. Write the name of each note in the square below it—then play and say the note names.

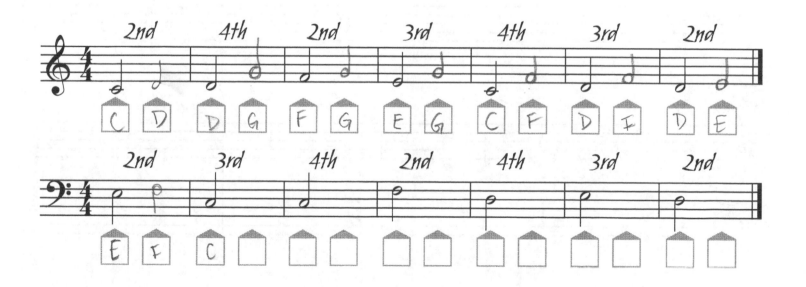

Play the RH & LH separately at first, then together.
Practice the RH *mf* and the LH *p*. The melody should
always be clearly heard above the accompaniment.

Practice Exercise: Sight Reading

Here's a Happy Song

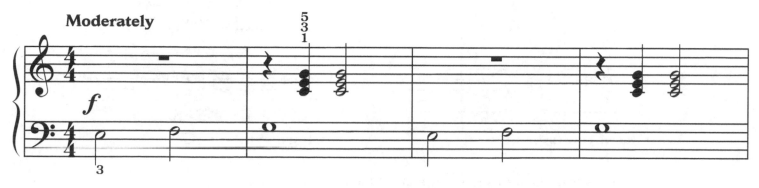

Practice Exercise: Sight Reading

B for Left Hand

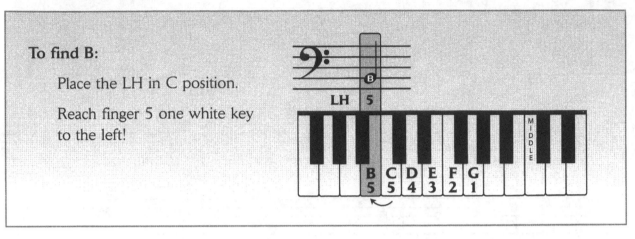

To find B:

Place the LH in C position.

Reach finger 5 one white key to the left!

Play slowly. Say the note names as you play.

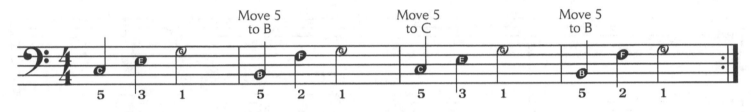

C Major and G7 Chords for Left Hand

Two frequently used chords are **C major** & **G7.**

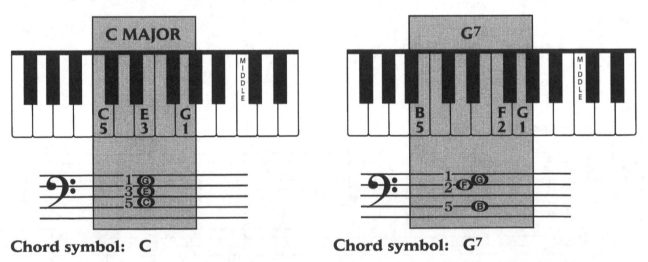

Chord symbol: C

Chord symbol: G7

Chord symbols are used in popular music to identify chord names.

Practice changing from the C chord to the G7 chord and back again:

1. The 1st finger plays G in both chords.
2. The 2nd finger plays F in the G7 chord.
3. Only the 5th finger moves out of C position (down to B) for G7.

Written Exercise: Away from the Keyboard

1. In the squares above the staff, write the names of the notes in each chord.

2. On the line below the staff, write the name of the chord (C or G7).

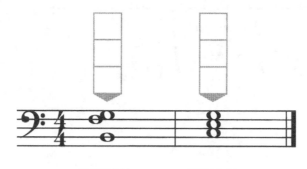

3. Circle each G7 chord.

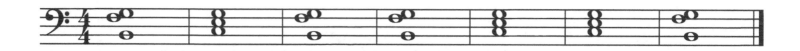

4. Connect the dots on the matching boxes.

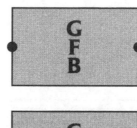

C
chord

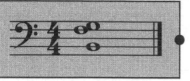

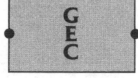

G7
chord

5. Write the name of each note in the square below it.

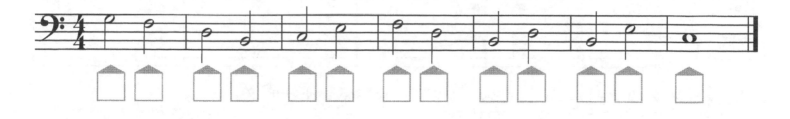

Tied Notes

When notes on the *same* line or space are joined with a curved line, they are called **tied notes**.

The key is held down for the *combined values* of both notes.

COUNT: "1 - 2 - 3 - 4 - | 1 - 2 - 3 - 4."

Merrily We Roll Along

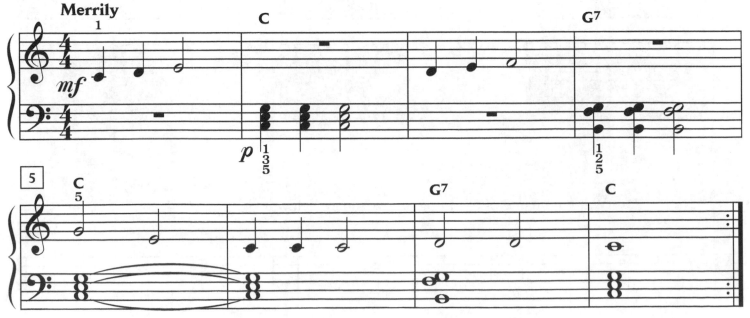

*In most popular sheet music, the chord symbols (C, G7, etc.) appear *above* the RH melody. The symbol appears *only* when the chord changes.

Largo
(from "The New World")

🔊 32

This famous melody (also known as Going Home) is from Dvořák's 9th Symphony written in 1893 when he was living in America. The first performance in Carnegie Hall was a triumph.

Antonin Dvořák
(1841–1904)

Practice Exercise: Sight Reading

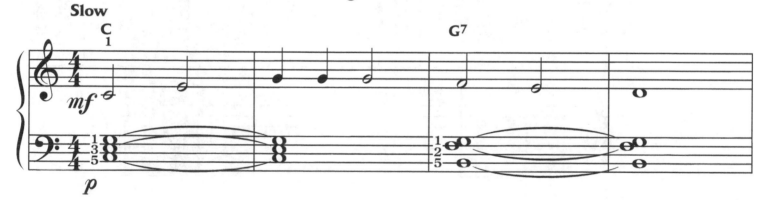

B for Right Hand

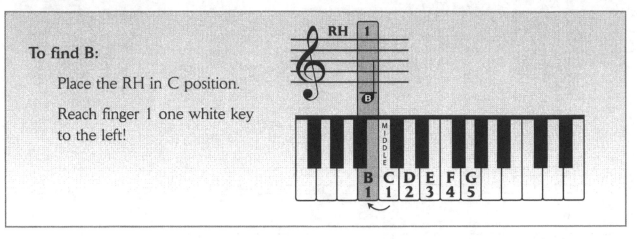

To find B:

Place the RH in C position.

Reach finger 1 one white key
to the left!

Play slowly. Say the note names as you play.

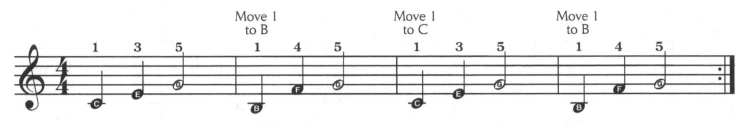

C Major and G7 Chords for Right Hand

It is very important to be able to play all chords with the *right* hand as well as the left.
Chords are used in either or both hands in popular and classical music.

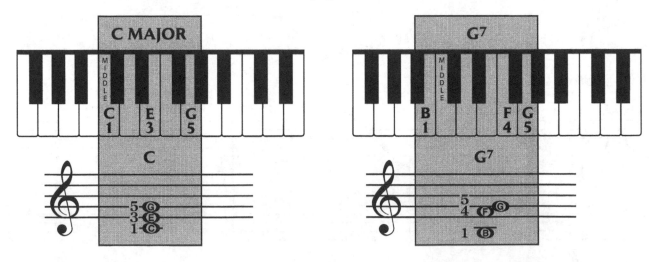

Practice changing from the C chord to the G7 chord and back again:

1. The 5th finger plays G in both chords.
2. The 4th finger plays F in the G7 chord.
3. Only the 1st finger moves out of C position (down to B) for G7.

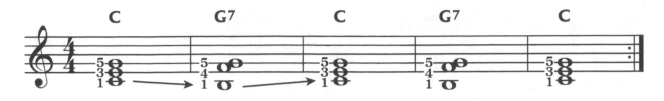

Written Exercise: Away from the Keyboard

1. In the squares above the staff, write the names of the notes in each chord.

2. On the line below the staff, write the name of the chord (C or G7).

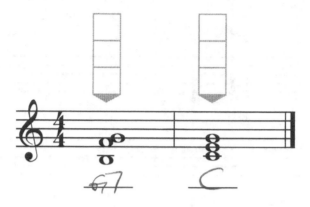

_G7_   _C_

3. Circle each G7 chord.

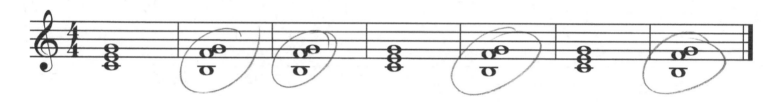

4. Connect the dots on the matching boxes.

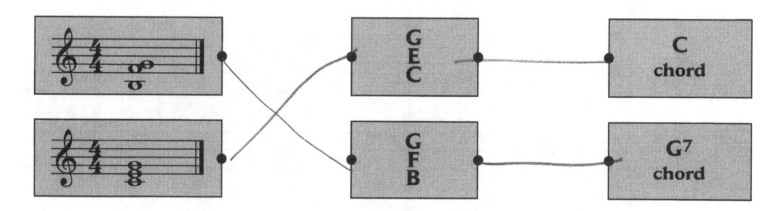

G E C   C chord

G F B   G7 chord

5. Write the name of each note in the square below it.

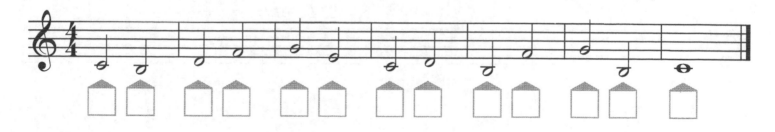

Practice Exercise: Sight Reading

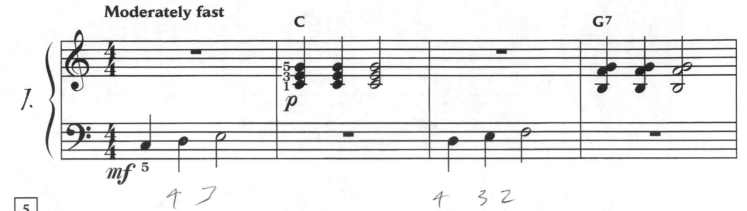

Mary Ann

Calypso tune

Moderately fast

All day, all night, Ma - ry Ann, (Ma - ry Ann,)

Down by the sea - shore, sift - in' sand; (sift - in' sand;)

All the lit - tle chil - dren love Ma - ry Ann, (Ma - ry Ann,)

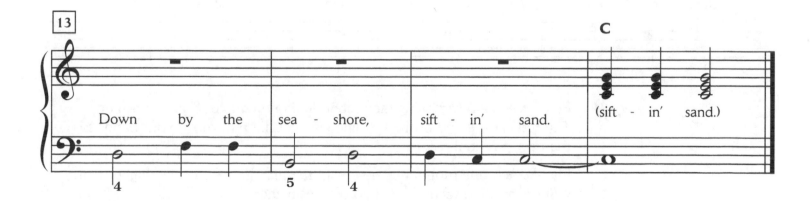

Down by the sea - shore, sift - in' sand. (sift - in' sand.)

Unit 7

New Time Signature, More Chords

Time Signature	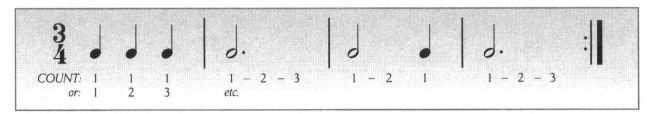

Review page 27.

Rhythm Exercise: Away from the Keyboard

Clap (or tap) the following rhythm. Clap *once* for each note, counting aloud.

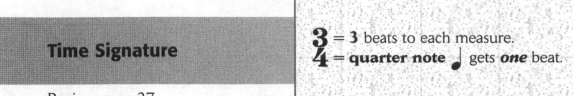

Rockets

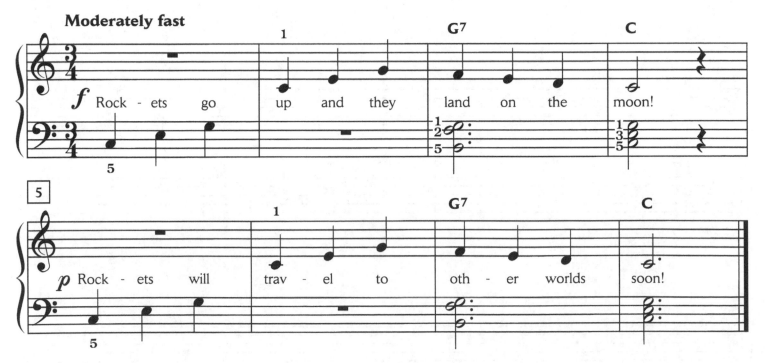

Important   Play *Rockets* again, playing the second line one **octave** (8 notes) higher. The rests at the end of the first line give you time to move your hands to the new position!

Play *Rockets* one more time, now with the first line one octave higher than written, and the second line two octaves higher.

This is excellent training in moving freely over the keyboard!

Sea Divers

Moderately slow

Down in the o - cean the sea div - ers go.

May - be they'll find man - y treas - ures be - low!

Important Play *Sea Divers* again, playing the second line one octave lower.

Optional: Play *Rockets* and *Sea Divers* as one piece, without skipping a beat when going from one to the other.

Slurs and Legato Playing

A **slur** is a curved line over or under notes on *different* lines or spaces.

Slurs mean play ***legato*** (smoothly connected).

Slurs often divide the music into **phrases.**
A phrase is a musical thought or sentence.

Practice Exercise: Sight Reading

Written Exercise: Away from the Keyboard

1. In the box above each note, write the number of counts it receives.
   The value of the notes in each measure of ¾ time must add up to 3!

2. Under each line, write *one note* equal in value to the sum of the *two* notes, as shown in the first example.

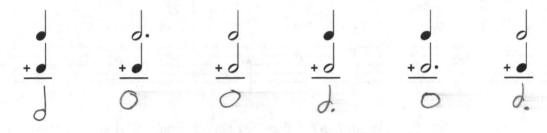

3. Under each line, write *one note* equal in value to the difference between the note(s) and rest, as shown in the first example.

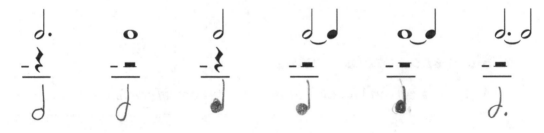

Rhythm Exercise: Away from the Keyboard

Clap (or tap) the following rhythms, counting aloud.

Write and Play Exercise

1. Draw a slur over the notes that are played for the second sentence of the lyrics.

2. Play the RH, counting aloud; then again, saying or singing the words. Connect the notes of each phrase as smoothly as you can.

3. Add chord symbols in the boxes above the treble staves—then play hands together.

Day Is Done

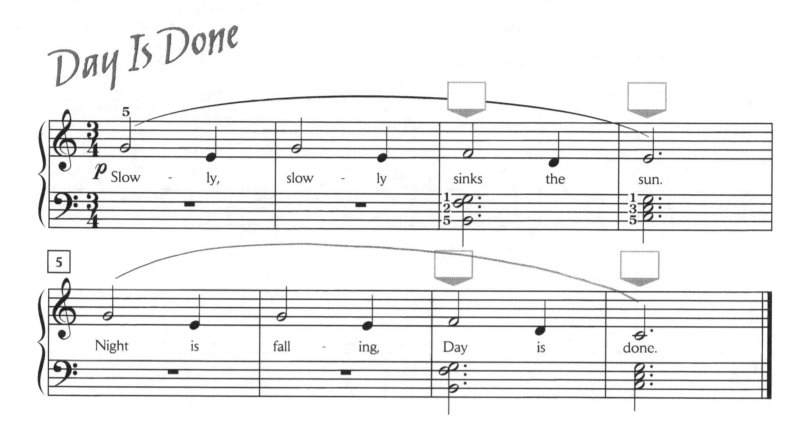

Slurs and Ties

If the notes are *different*—it's a **slur.** If the notes are the *same*—it's a **tie.**

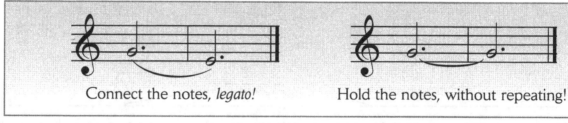

Connect the notes, *legato!*   Hold the notes, without repeating!

4. Write *tie* or *slur* in the box under each pair of notes, as shown in the first box:

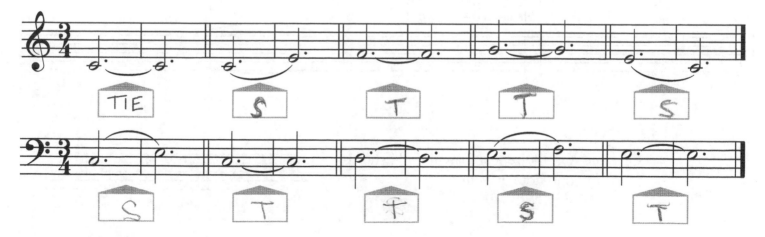

American Folk Song

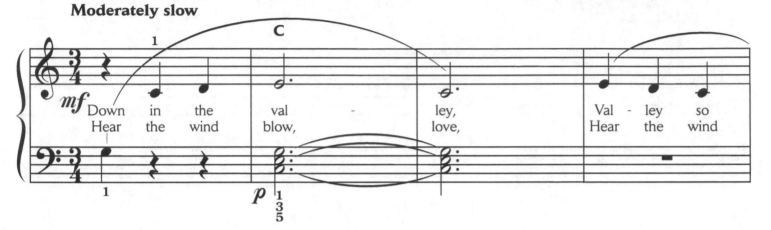

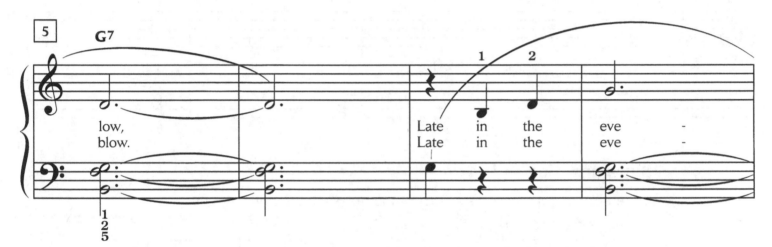

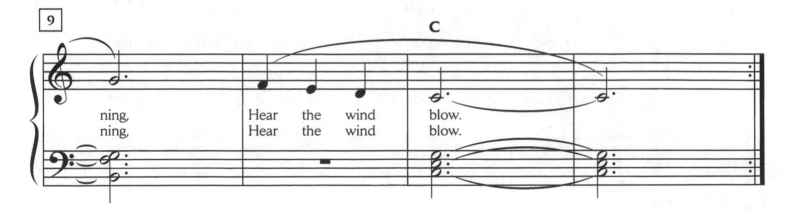

Optional: On the repeat, play the LH chords
one note at a time.

What Can I Share?

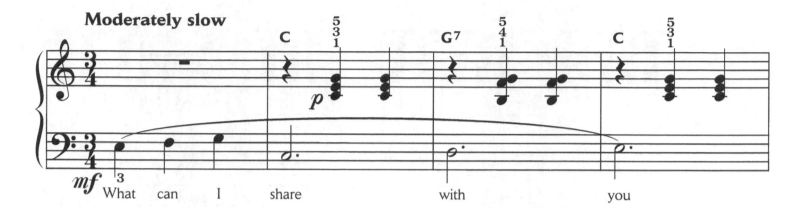

Moderately slow

What can I share with you

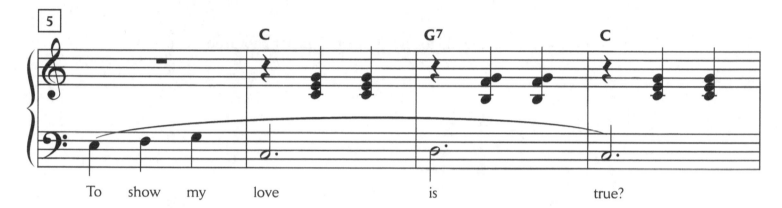

To show my love is true?

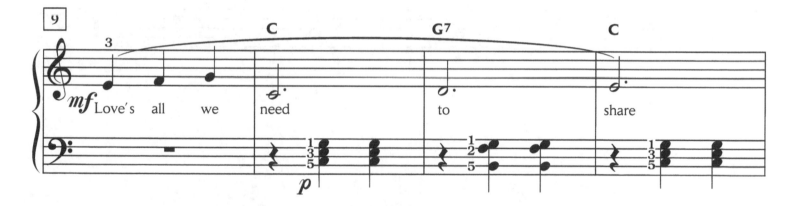

Love's all we need to share

To show how much we care!

C Major and F Major Chords for Left Hand

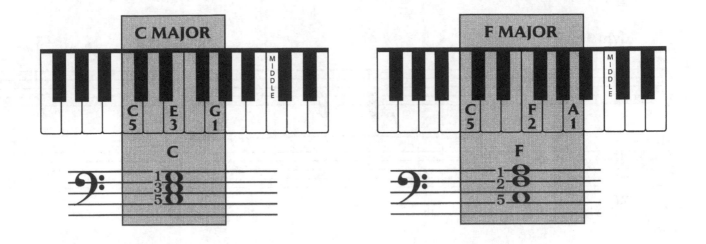

The C major chord is frequently followed by the F major chord, and vice-versa.

Play slowly.

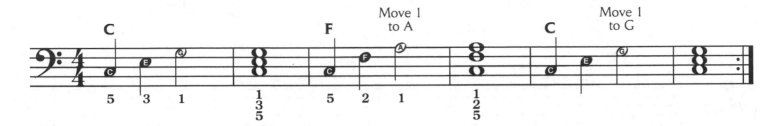

Practice changing from the C chord to the F chord and back again:

1. The 5th finger plays C in both chords.
2. The 2nd finger plays F in the F chord.
3. Only the 1st finger moves out of C position (up to A) for the F chord.

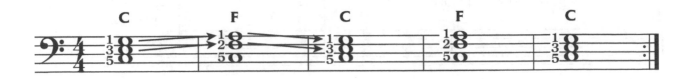

Practice Exercise: Sight Reading

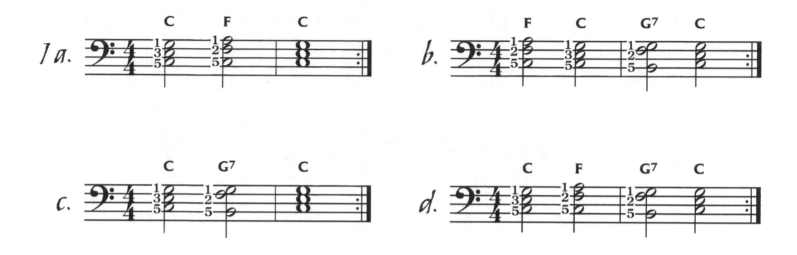

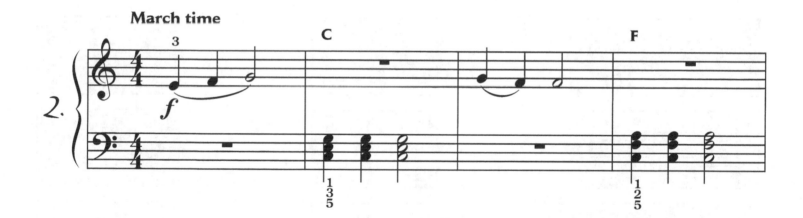

Written Exercise: Away from the Keyboard

1. In the squares above the staff, write the names of the notes in each chord.

2. On the line below the staff, write the name of the chord (C, F or G7).

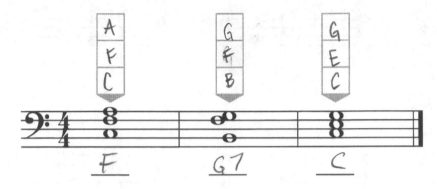

3. Circle each F major chord.

4. Connect the dots on the matching boxes.

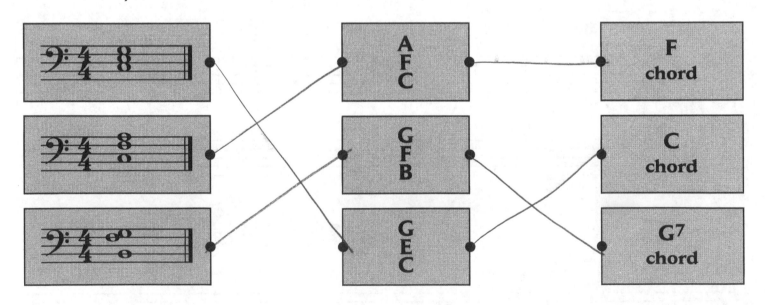

5. Write the name of each note in the square below it.

Use after page 45.

JAZZ WALTZ

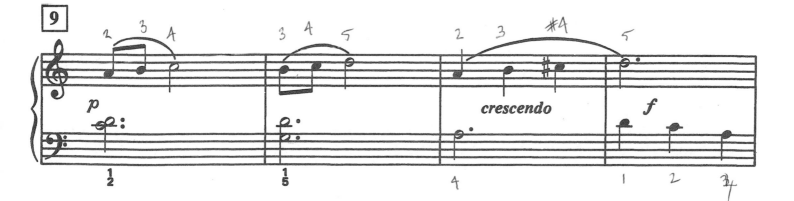

When the Saints Go Marching In

(with RH Melody
& LH Chords)

Incomplete Measure Some pieces begin with an incomplete measure. The first measure of this piece has only 3 counts. The missing count is found in the last measure! When you repeat the whole song, you will have one whole measure of 4 counts when you play the last measure plus the first measure.

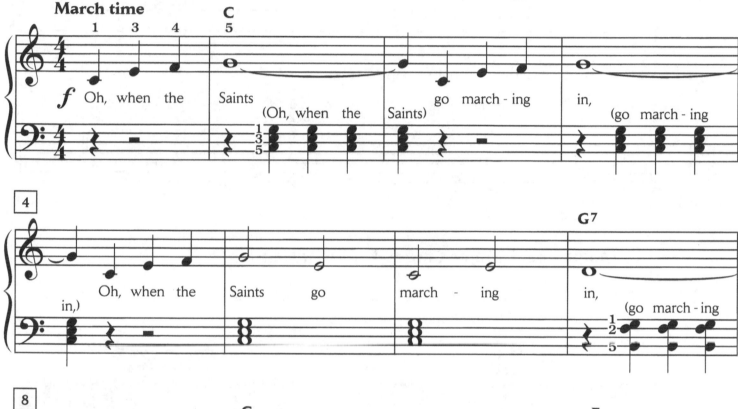

March time

Oh, when the Saints go march-ing in, (Oh, when the Saints) go march-ing in, (go march-ing

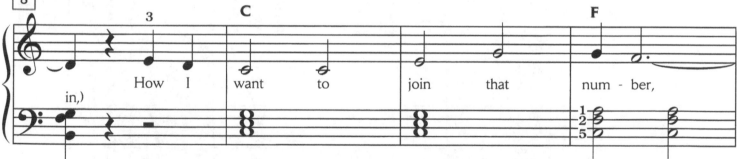

4

in,) Oh, when the Saints go march - ing in, (go march-ing

8

in,) How I want to join that num - ber,

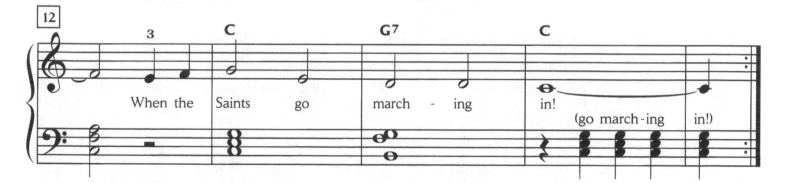

12

When the Saints go march - ing in! (go march-ing in!)

A for Right Hand

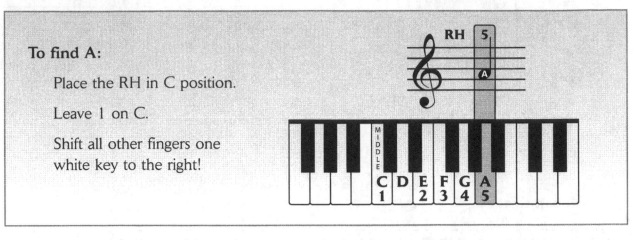

To find A:

Place the RH in C position.

Leave 1 on C.

Shift all other fingers one
white key to the right!

Play slowly. Say the note names as you play.

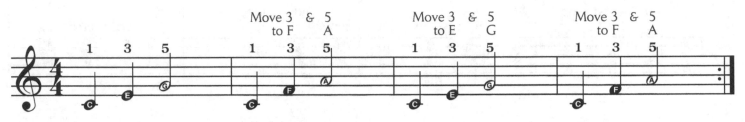

C Major and F Major Chords for Right Hand

Notice that *two* fingers must move to the right when changing from
the C major chord to the F major chord.

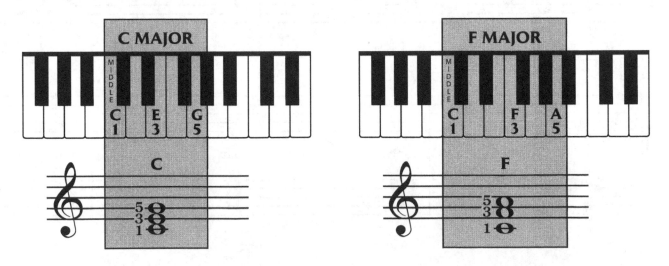

Practice changing from the C chord to the F chord and back again:

1. The 1st finger plays C in both chords.
2. The 3rd finger moves up to F and the 5th finger moves up to A for the F chord.

Practice Exercise: **Sight Reading**

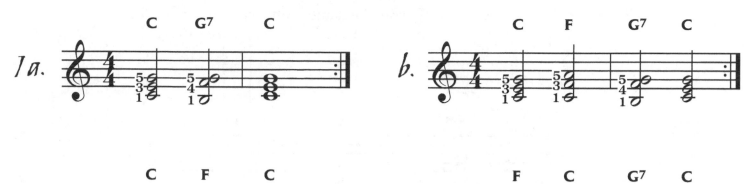

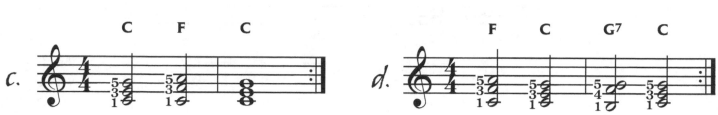

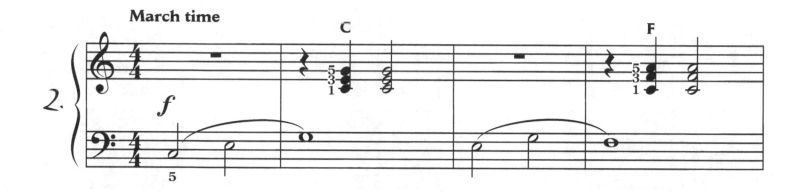

Written Exercise: Away from the Keyboard

1. In the squares above the staff, write the names of the notes in each chord.

2. On the line below the staff, write the name of the chord (C, F or G7).

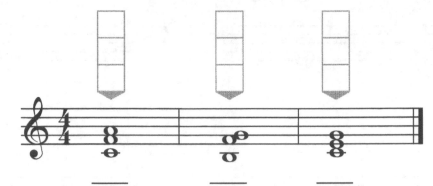

3. Circle each F major chord.

4. Connect the dots on the matching boxes.

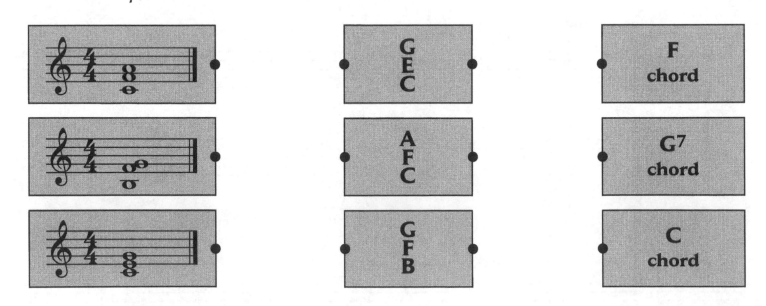

5. Write the name of each note in the square below it.

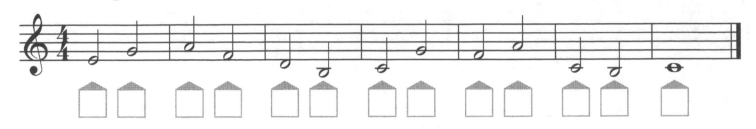

When the Saints Go Marching In

(with LH Melody
& RH Chords)

The origin of this famous spiritual is uncertain, although it may
have come from the Bahamas. Rumors say that the spiritual
was played in New Orleans at funerals near the turn of the
century, at a slow tempo* on the way to the cemetery and at a
fast tempo returning from the cemetery.

March time

After you have learned both versions of *When the Saints Go Marching In,* you will find it very
effective to play page 81 followed immediately by page 85. Instead of playing the piece one
way and repeating, you will be playing the melody first in the RH, then in the LH!

tempo = speed

Old Country Music

This charming country song reviews all the chords and many of the notes, dynamics and other musical symbols previously introduced.

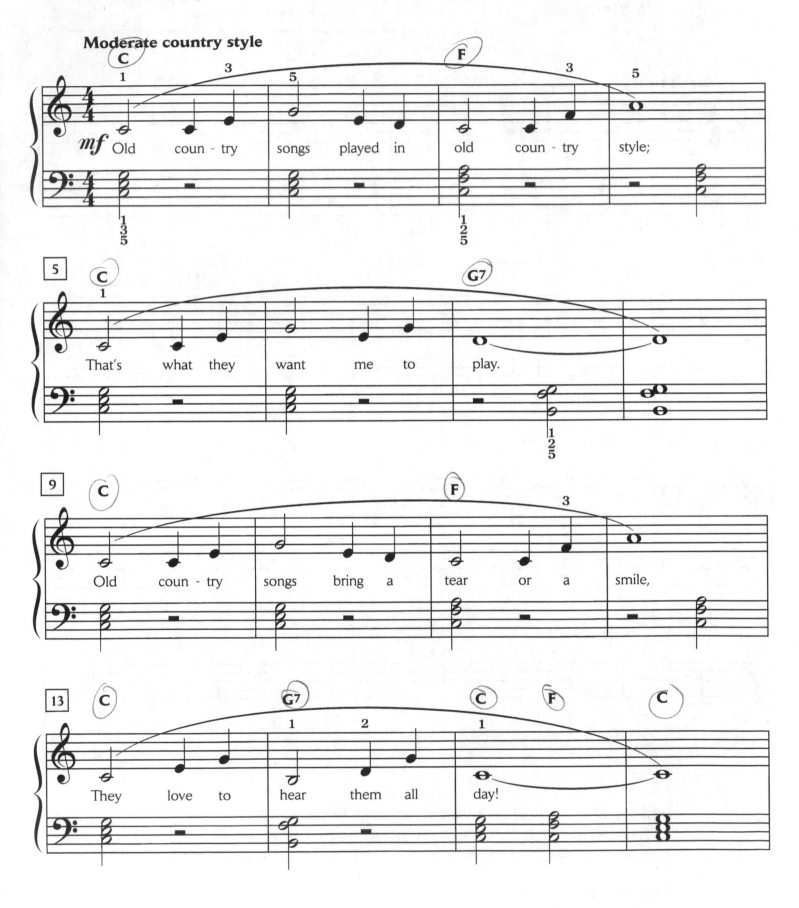

Moderate country style

Old coun-try songs played in old coun-try style;

That's what they want me to play.

Old coun-try songs bring a tear or a smile,

They love to hear them all day!

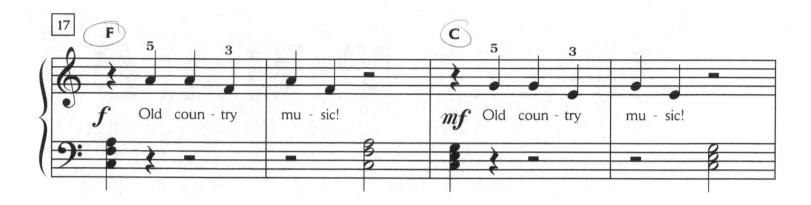

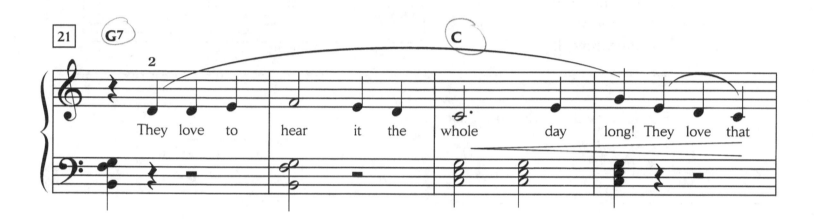

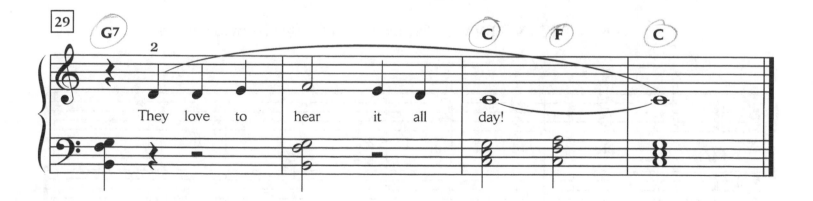

Unit 8

G Position, The Sharp Sign

The **G Position** is another new position—it uses four new notes.

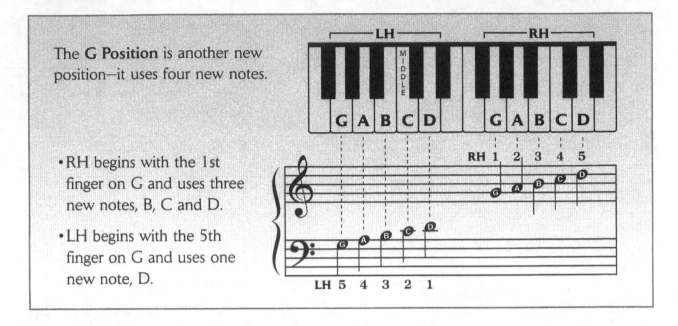

- RH begins with the 1st finger on G and uses three new notes, B, C and D.

- LH begins with the 5th finger on G and uses one new note, D.

Play and say the note names. Do this several times!

Intervals in G Position

1. **MELODIC INTERVALS** Say the name of each interval as you play.

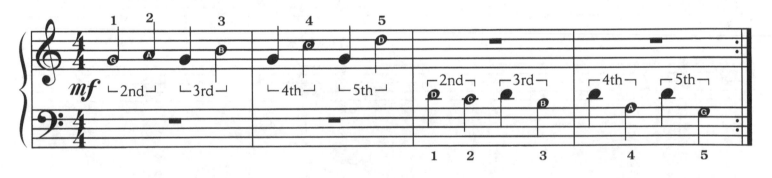

2. **HARMONIC INTERVALS** Say the name of each interval as you play.

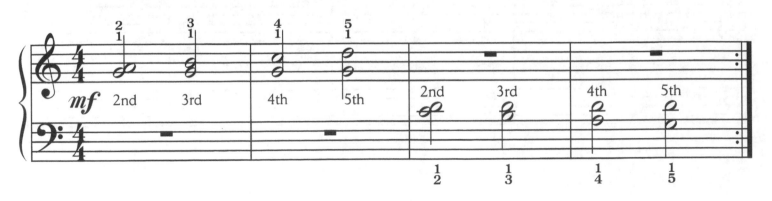

Write and Play Exercise

1. Write the names of the notes in the boxes—then play.

The Bandleader

Moderately fast, like a march

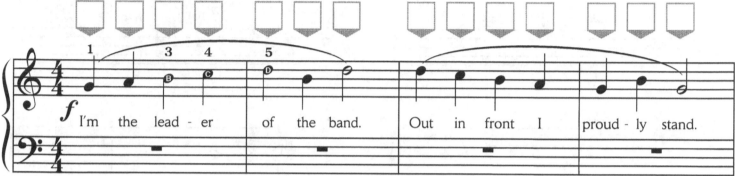

f I'm the lead - er   of the band.   Out in front I   proud - ly stand.

All   I   do   is   wave   my   hand;   Out comes mu - sic   loud   and   grand!

2. Write the name of each note in the square below it—then play and say the note names.

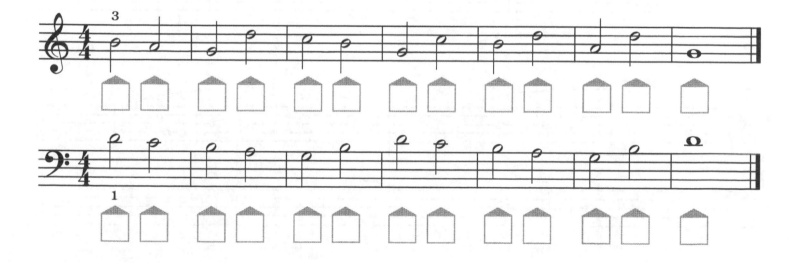

Practice Exercise: Sight Reading

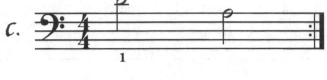

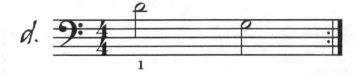

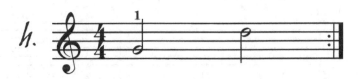

Moderately slow

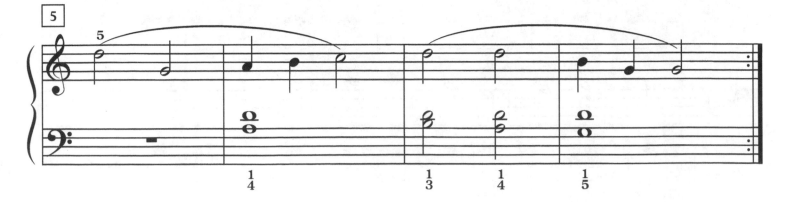

Before playing hands together, play LH alone, naming each harmonic interval!

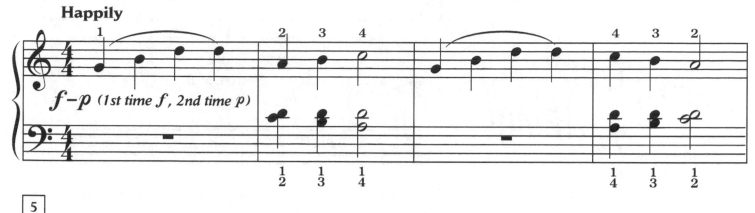

Before playing hands together, play LH alone, naming each harmonic interval!

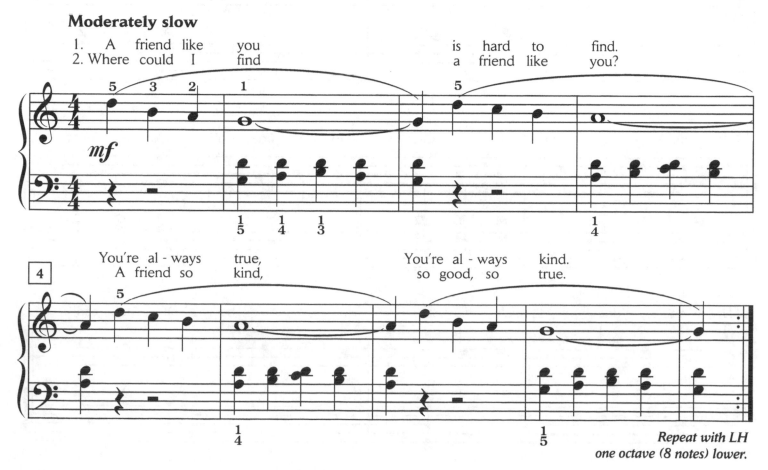

Sharp Sign ♯

The **sharp sign** before a note means play the next key to the *right,* whether black or white!

When a sharp (♯) appears before a note, it applies to that note for the rest of the measure!

Write and Play Exercise

1. In the boxes above the keyboard, write the names of the indicated sharp keys.

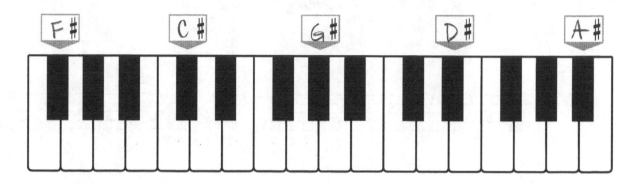

When writing sharp signs, be sure the *center* of the sign is on the line or space of the note to be sharped: ♯ ♯

2. Change each note below to a sharp note. Write the sharp sign *before* the note!

3. Write the name of each note in the box above it.

4. Play the notes, using RH 3 or LH 3.

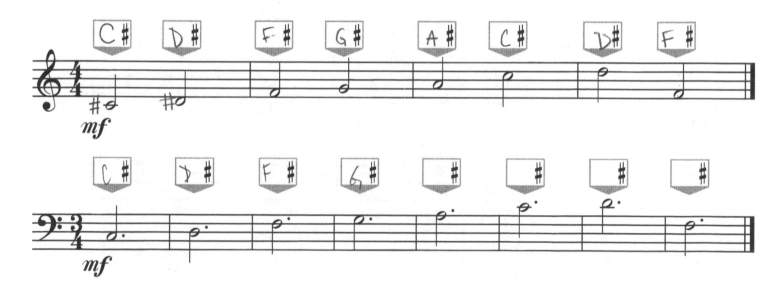

Practice Exercise: Sight Reading

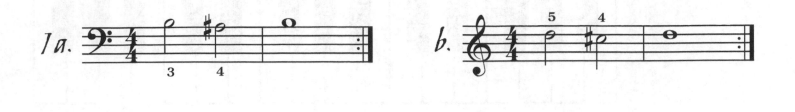

Moderately fast

Will You, Won't You?

Adapted from "Alice in Wonderland,"
by Lewis Carroll

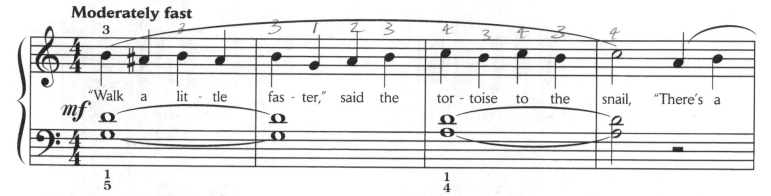

Moderately fast

"Walk a lit - tle fas - ter," said the tor - toise to the snail, "There's a

por - poise close be - hind me, and he's tread - ing on my tail!"

A little faster, very rhythmically

Will you, won't you, will you, won't you, will you join the dance?

Will you, won't you, will you, won't you, Won't you join the dance?

Unit 9

Chords in G Position

G Major and D7 Chords for Left Hand

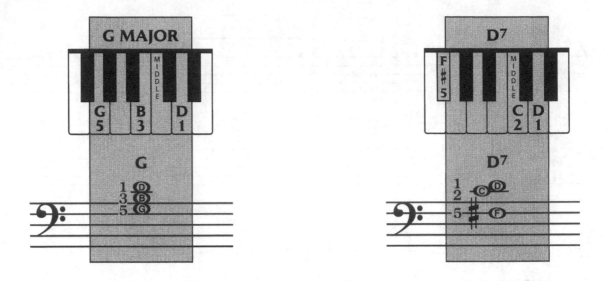

The G major chord is frequently followed by the D7 chord, and vice-versa.

Play slowly.

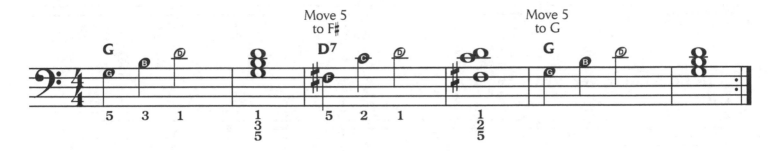

Practice changing from the G chord to the D7 chord and back again:

1. The 1st finger plays D in both chords.
2. The 2nd finger plays C in the D7 chord.
3. Only the 5th finger moves out of G position (down to F♯) for D7.

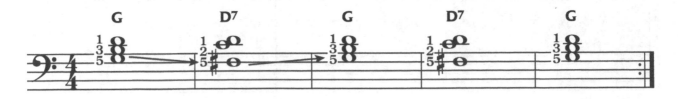

Use after page 33.

DREAMING

Gently *2nd time play one octave higher*

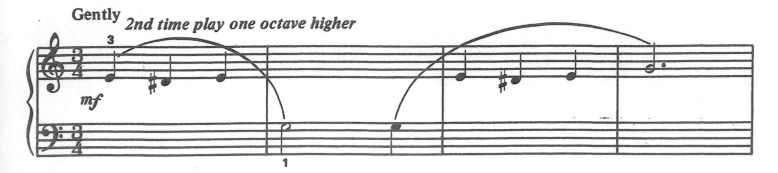

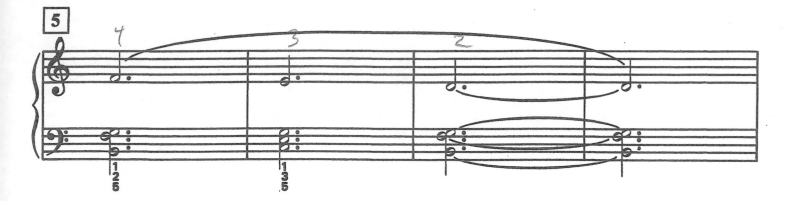

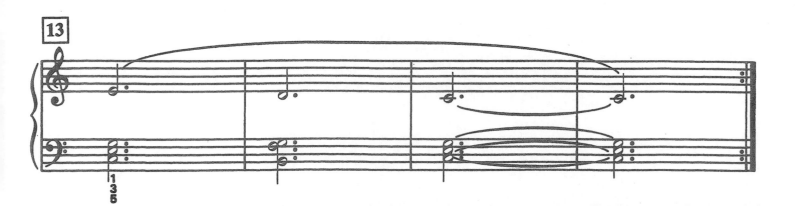

Practice Exercise: Sight Reading

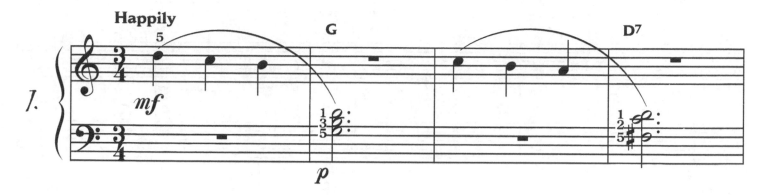

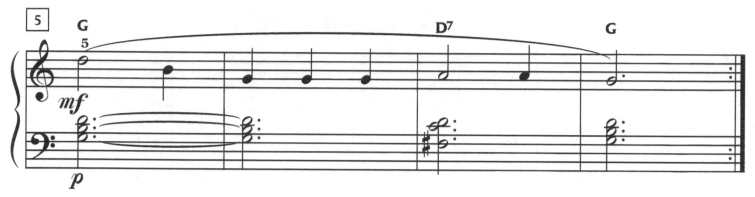

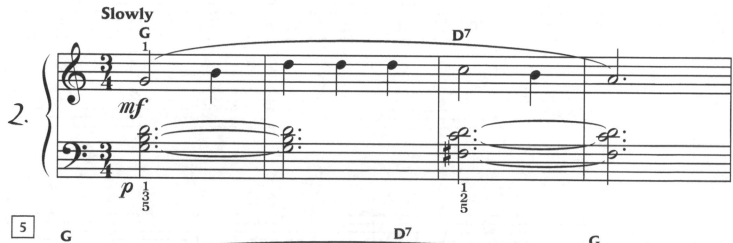

The Cuckoo

Happily

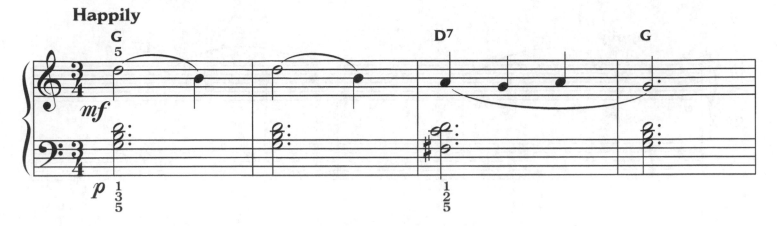

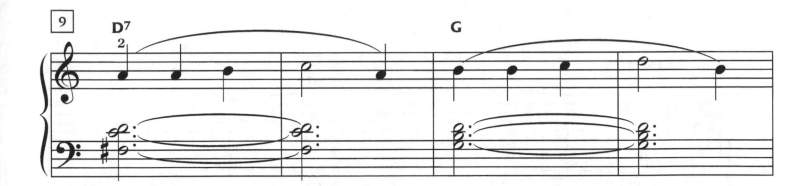

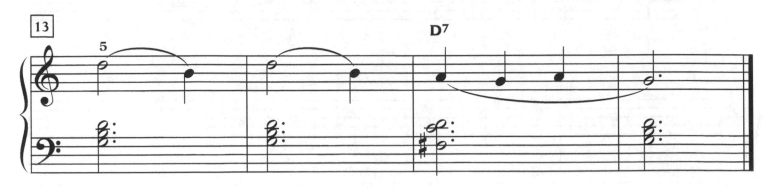

Optional: Play the LH chords one note at a time.

Write and Play Exercise

1. Write the chord symbols (G or D7) in the boxes below.

2. Play & count.

3. Play & say the chord names.

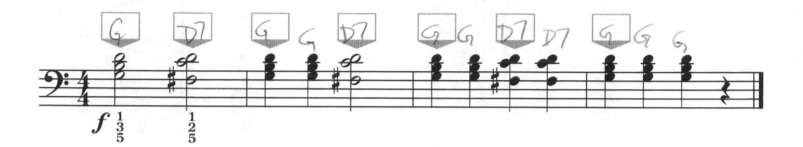

4. Write the chord symbols in the boxes below.

5. Play & count.

6. Play & sing (or say) the words.

Liza Jane

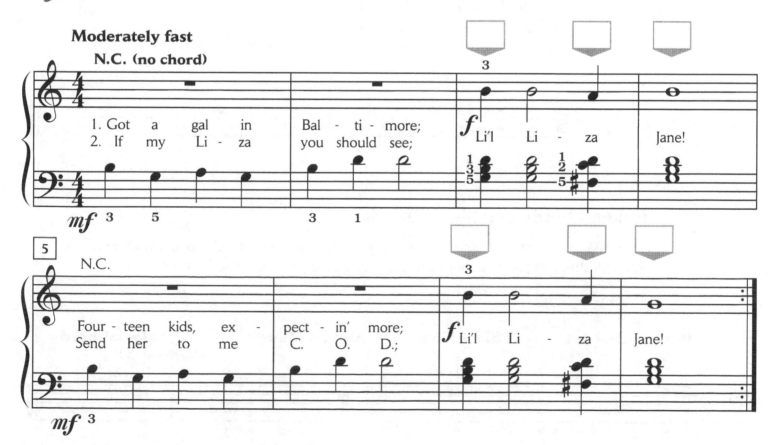

G Major and D7 Chords for Right Hand

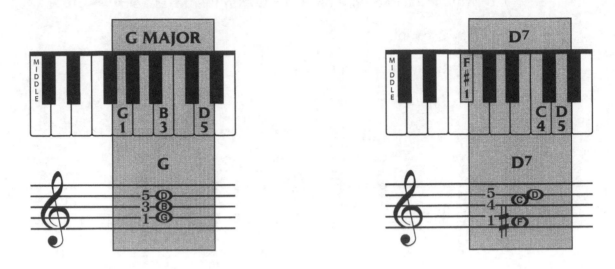

Play slowly.

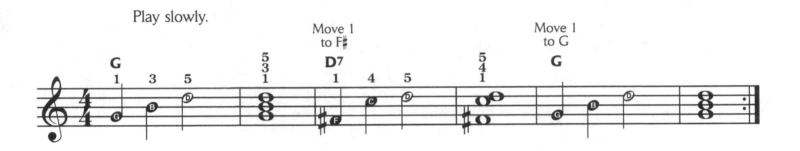

Practice changing from the G chord to the D7 chord and back again:

1. The 5th finger plays D in both chords.
2. The 4th finger plays C in the D7 chord.
3. Only the 1st finger moves out of G position (down to F♯) for D7.

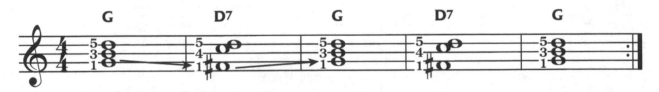

Broken Chords and Block Chords

When the three notes of a chord are played separately, it is called a **broken chord.**
When all three notes of a chord are played together, it is called a **block chord.**

Play several times:

Practice Exercise: Sight Reading

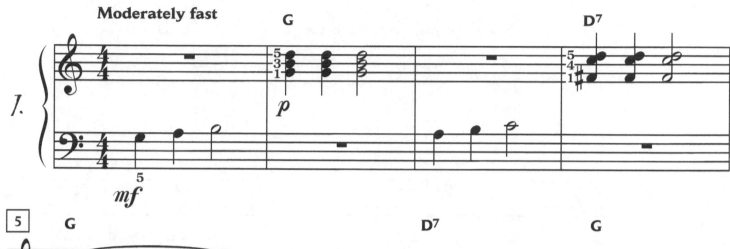

Written Exercise: Away from the Keyboard

1. In the squares above the staff, write the names of the notes in each chord.

2. On the line below the staff, write the name of the chord (G or D7).

3. Circle each D7 chord.

4. Write the name of each note in the square below it.

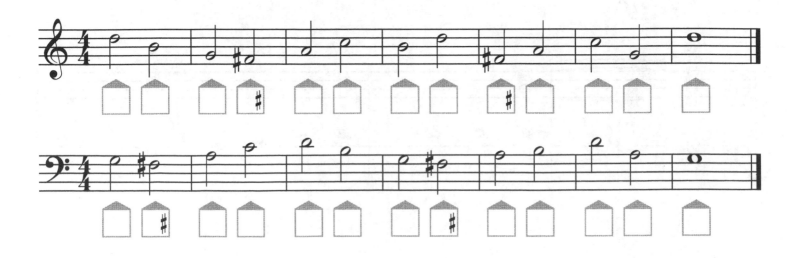

I Know Where I'm Goin'

Scotch-Irish Folk Song

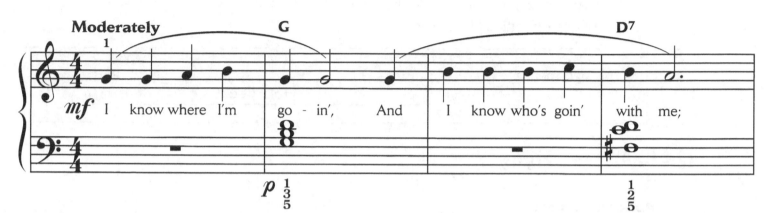

I know where I'm go-in', And I know who's goin' with me;

I know who I love, And I know who I'll mar-ry.

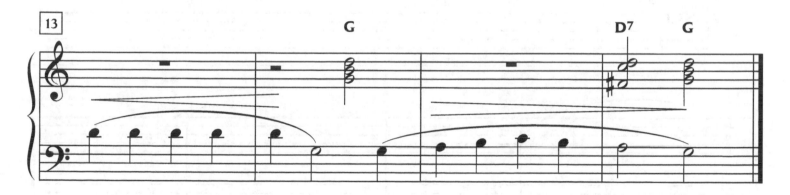

The Damper Pedal

The *right* pedal is called the **damper pedal.** When you hold the damper pedal down, any tone you sound will continue after you release the key. See page 12.

- Use the right foot on the damper pedal.
- Always keep your heel on the floor.
- Use your ankle like a hinge.

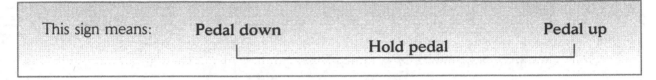

This sign means: **Pedal down**   **Pedal up**

Hold pedal

Practice Exercise: Sight Reading

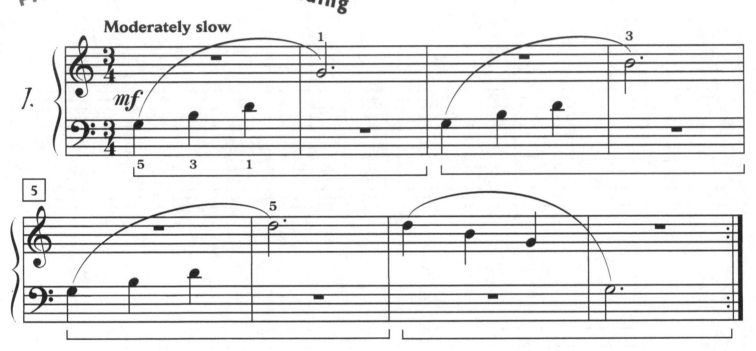

1.

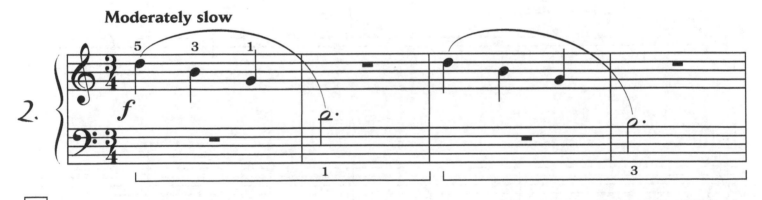

Many pieces are made entirely of broken chords, as this one is.

Harp Song

Optional:

1. Play the third and fourth measures of each line one octave higher than written.
2. Play the first and second measures of each line one octave lower than written.

E for Left Hand

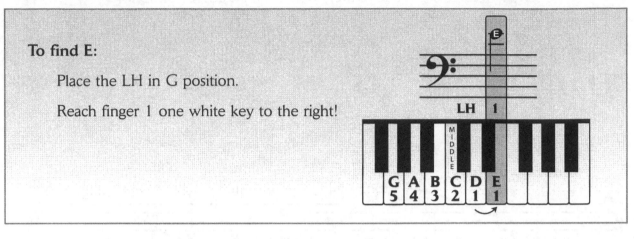

To find E:

Place the LH in G position.

Reach finger 1 one white key to the right!

Play slowly. Say the note names as you play.

A New Position of the C Major Chord

You have already played the C major chord with C as the lowest note: C E G.
When you play these same three notes in any order, you still have a C major chord.
When you are playing in G position, it is most convenient to play G as the lowest note: G C E.

The following diagrams show how easy it is to move from the G major chord to the
C major chord, when G is the lowest note of both chords.

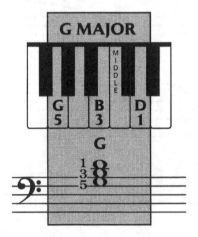

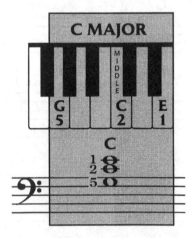

Practice changing from the G chord to the C chord and back again:

1. The 5th finger plays G in both chords.
2. The 2nd finger plays C in the C chord.
3. Only the 1st finger moves out of G position (up to E) for the C chord.

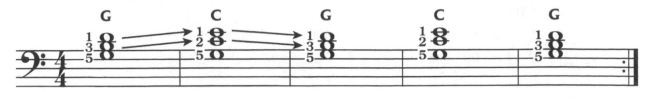

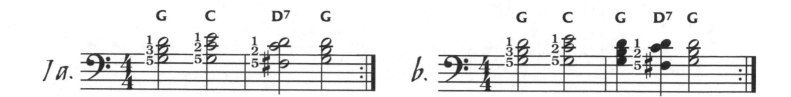

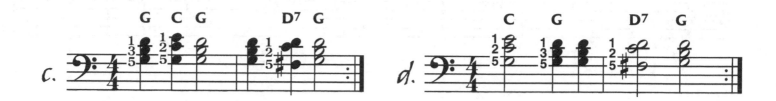

Write and Play Exercise

1. Write the chord symbols (G, C or D7) in the boxes below.

2. Play & count.

3. Play & say the chord names.

In addition to playing the notes separately in broken chords, you may also play one note followed by the remaining two notes played together.

4. Write the chord symbols in the boxes below. You will have to look at all the notes in each measure to determine the chord name.

5. Play & say the chord names.

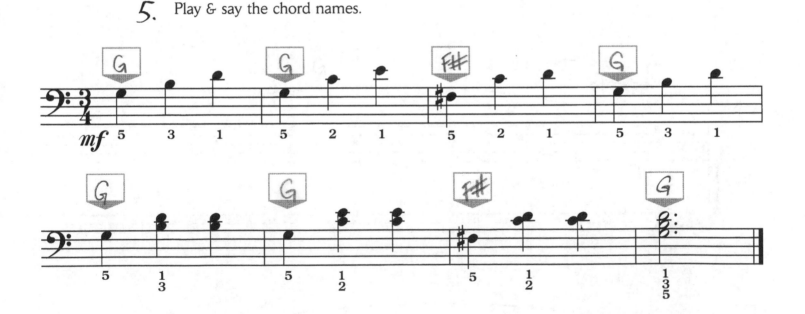

Practice Exercise: Technic

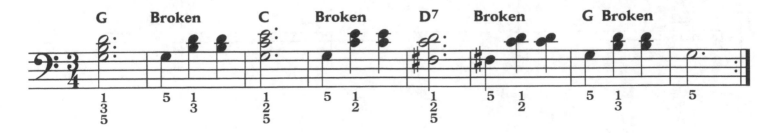

Beautiful Brown Eyes

E for Right Hand

To find E:

Place the RH in G position.

Leave finger 1 on G.

Shift all other fingers one white key to the right!

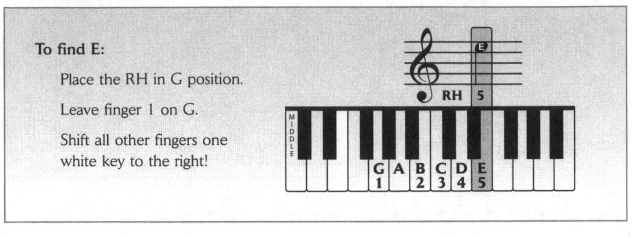

Play slowly. Say the note names as you play.

New C Major Chord Position for Right Hand

Notice that *two* fingers must move to the right when changing from the G major chord to the C major chord.

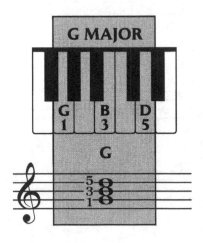
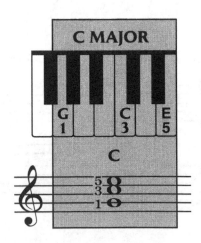

Practice changing from the G chord to the C chord and back again:

1. The 1st finger plays G in both chords.
2. The 3rd finger moves up to C and the 5th finger moves up to E for the C chord.

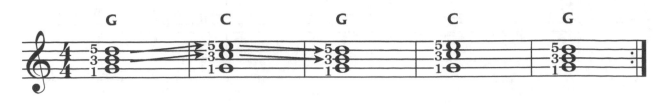

Practice Exercise: Sight Reading

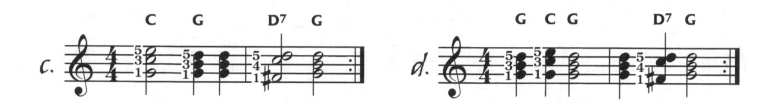

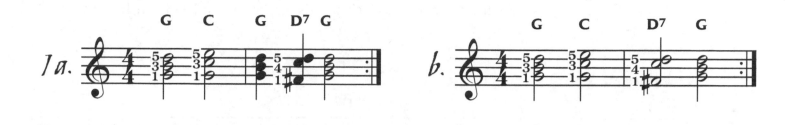

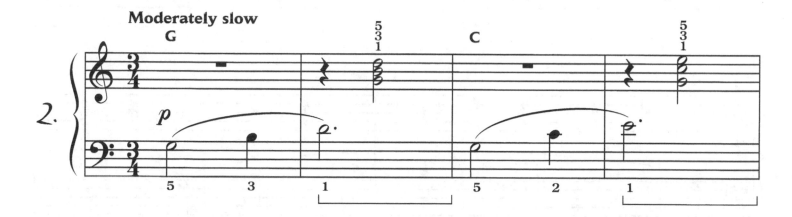

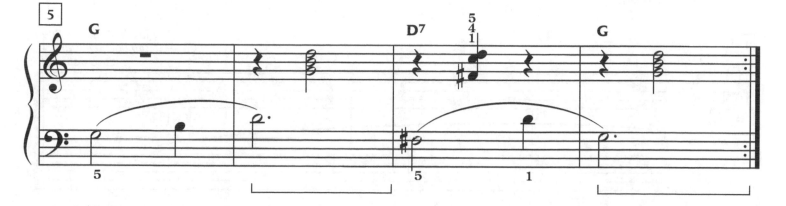

Alpine Melody

The LH melody of this piece consists entirely of broken chords, which are the same as the block chords played by the RH in each measure!

Moderately slow

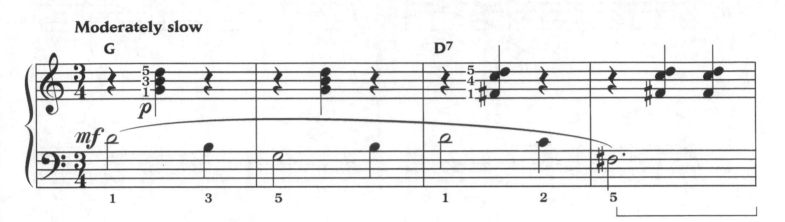

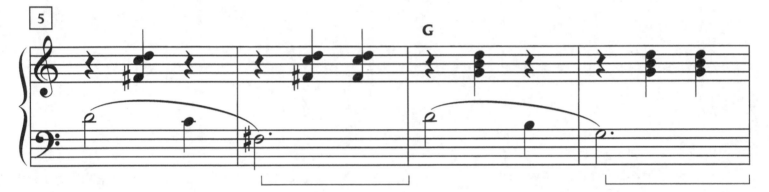

Play both hands 8va (one octave higher) the 2nd time!

Written Exercise: Away from the Keyboard

1. In the squares above the staff, write the names of the notes in each chord.

2. On the line below the staff, write the name of the chord (G, C or D7).

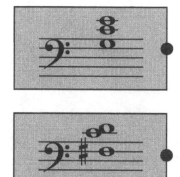

3. Connect the dots on the matching boxes.

D
C
F#

E
C
G

D
B
G

C

G

D⁷

4. Write the name of each note in the square below it.

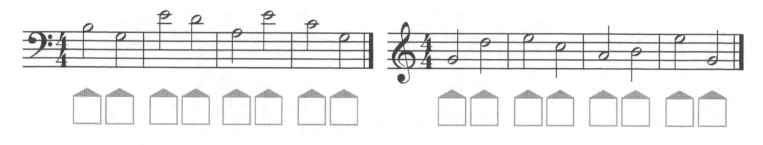

Unit 10

The Flat Sign, Eighth Notes, Dotted Quarter Notes

Flat Sign ♭

The **flat sign** before a note means play the next key to the *left,* whether black or white!

When a flat (♭) appears before a note, it applies to that note for the rest of the measure!

Rock It Away!

Moderately fast

Practice Exercise: **Sight Reading**

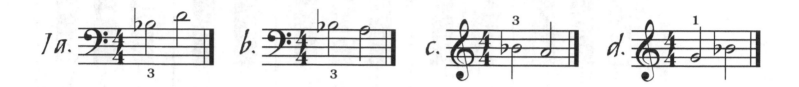

Write and Play Exercise

1. In the boxes above the keyboard, write the names of the indicated flat keys.

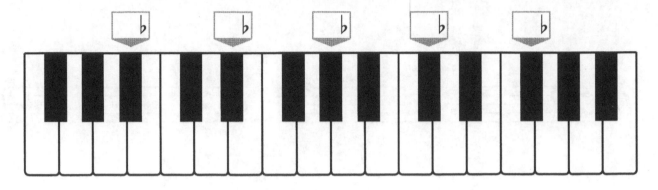

When writing flat signs, be sure to *center* the sign on the line or space of the note to be flatted:

2. Change each note below to a flat note. Write the flat sign *before* the note!

3. Write the name of each note in the box above it.

4. Play the notes, using RH 3 or LH 3.

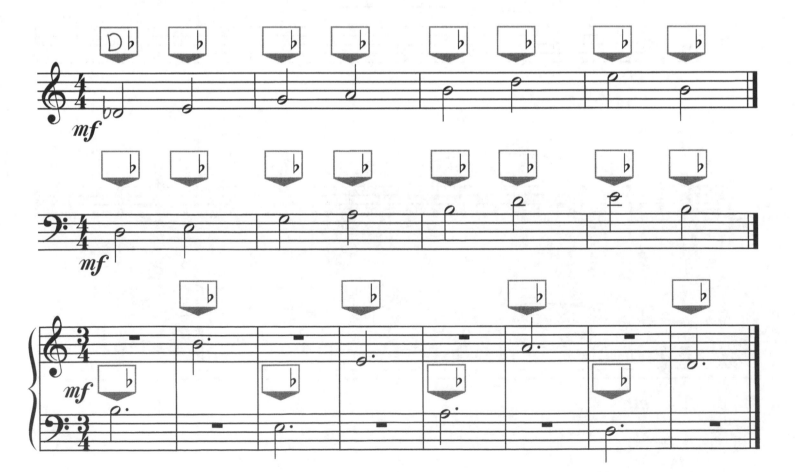

Für Ludwig

This piece is based on one of Ludwig van Beethoven's most famous compositions, Für Elise (For Elise). Beethoven dedicated many of his compositions to women. Some were dedicated to women of nobility, but most of them were offered as mementos to women to whom he was particularly attracted.

Not too fast, but with great optimism

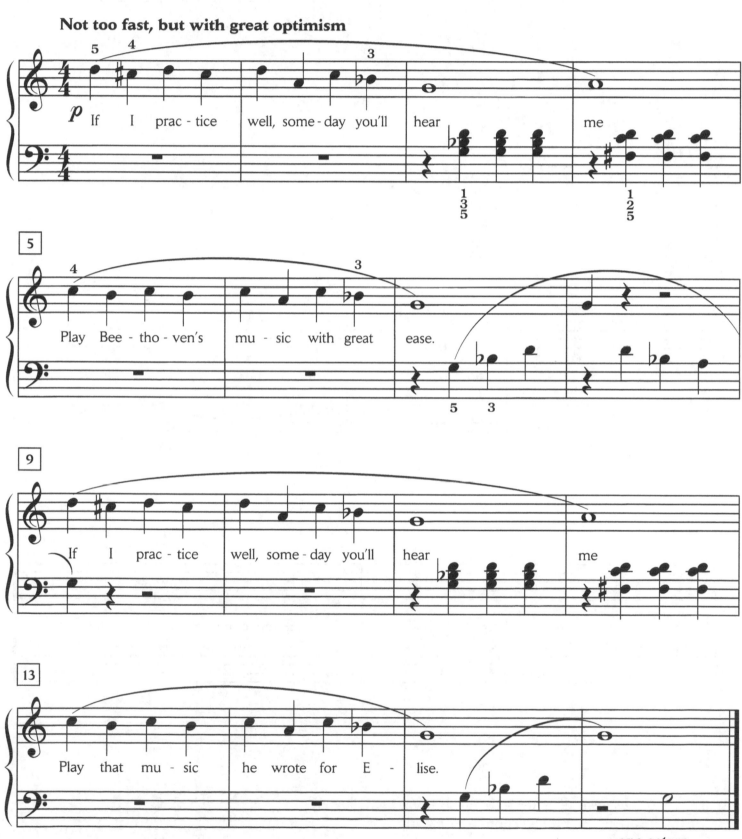

*one octave
lower than written*

Fermata

This sign is called
a **fermata**.

Hold the note under the
fermata *longer* than its value.

Shoo, Fly, Shoo!

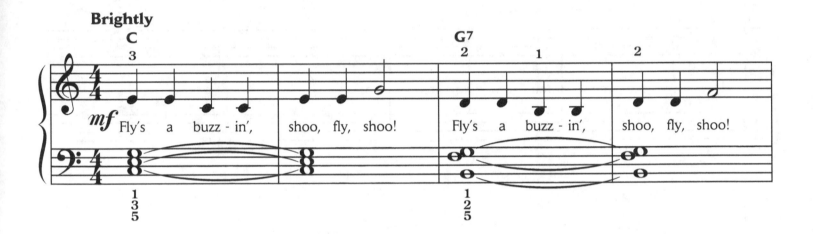

Optional: Play the LH chords using the following
broken-chord accompaniment.

Eighth Notes

Two **eighth notes** are played in the time of one quarter note.

Eighth notes are usually played in pairs.

COUNT: "1   &"
or: "two   eighths"

When a piece contains eighth notes, count:

"1 - &" or "quar - ter"   for each quarter note;

"1 - &" or "two eighths" for each pair of eighth notes.

Rhythm Exercise: Away from the Keyboard

Clap (or tap) the following rhythm, counting aloud.

COUNT: 1 & 1 & 1 & 1 &   1 & 1 & 1 & 1 &
or: 1 & 2 & 3 & 4 &   1 & 2 & 3 & 4 &

Skip to My Lou

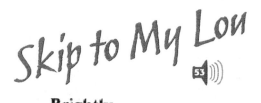

The melody of *Skip to My Lou* is the same as *Shoo, Fly, Shoo!* except for the eighth notes.

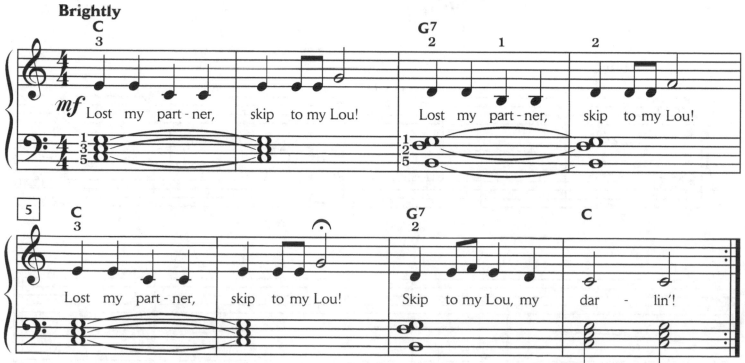

Optional: Play the LH chords using the following broken-chord accompaniment.

Rhythm Exercise: Away from the Keyboard

Clap (or tap) the following rhythms, counting aloud.

Practice Exercise: Sight Reading

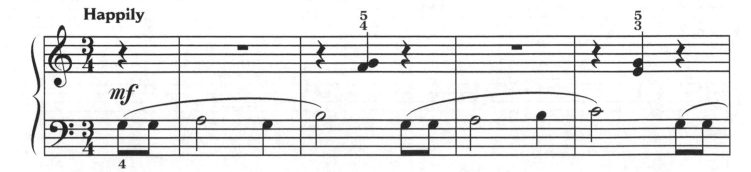

Standing in the Need of Prayer

54

D. C. al Fine

D. C. al Fine (Da Capo al Fine) means *repeat from the beginning and play to the end (Fine).*

Rhythmically , not too fast

D. C. al Fine

Combining Middle C Position and C Position

You are now ready to play music that involves more than one position. This piece begins with the hands in Middle C Position. After the first full measure is played, the LH moves to C Position to play chords. Change positions as indicated in the music.

The Gift to Be Simple

This beautiful old Shaker melody was used by the famous American composer, Aaron Copland, in his well-known symphonic composition, Appalachian Spring.

Folk melody

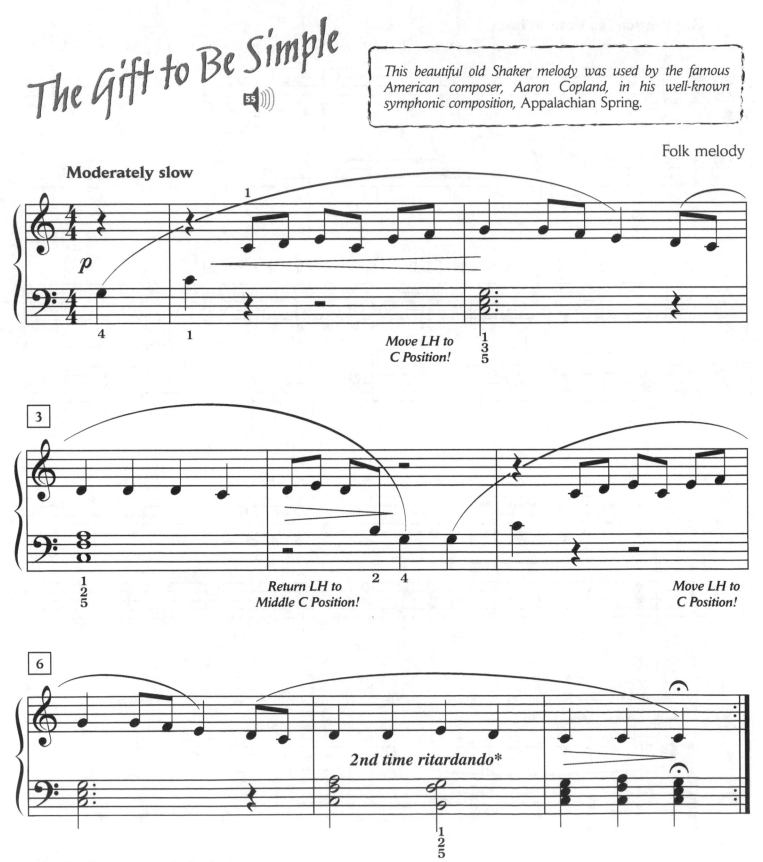

ritardando means *gradually slowing.*

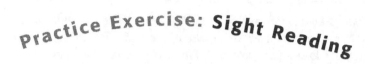

Practice Exercise: Sight Reading

Moderately slow

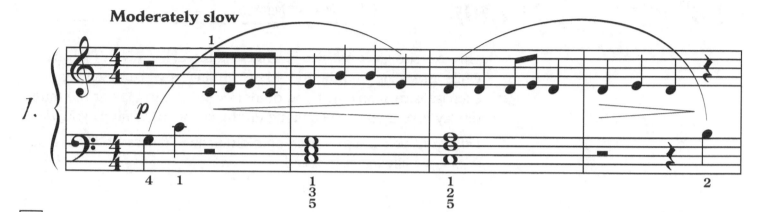

Rhythmically, not too fast

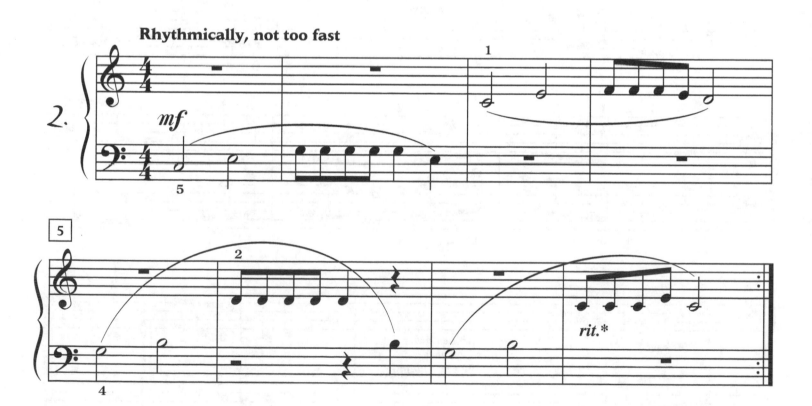

rit. = abbreviation for *ritardando*

Technic Exercise: Warm-Ups

The Amazing Aerobics of Hanon

No. 1

Charles-Louis Hanon (1819–1900) wrote, "The 4th and 5th fingers are almost useless because of the lack of special exercises to strengthen them." He then proceeded to devise some exercises which were so successful that they brought him worldwide fame.

This exercise gives practice in stretching the LH 4th & 5th fingers while ascending, and the RH 4th & 5th fingers while descending. The exercise is so simple that you do not even have to look at the music to play it, and you can continue up the keyboard as far as you wish.

Lift fingers high and play each note distinctly. Practice slowly at first, then gradually increase speed.

Moderately slow to Moderately fast

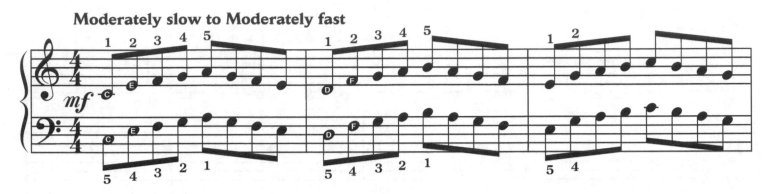

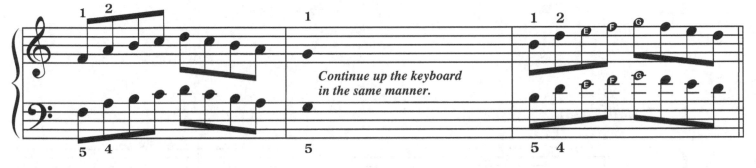

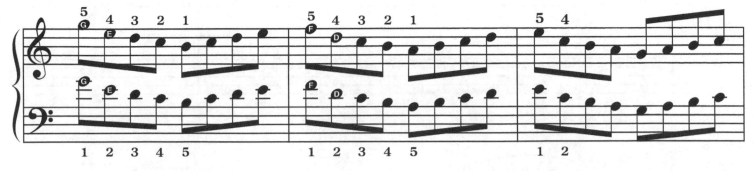

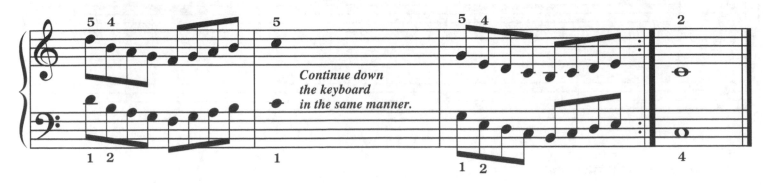

No. 2

This exercise from the Hanon series uses the same system as the previous one for moving up and down the keyboard. It not only continues the stretch between the 5th and 4th fingers, but also strengthens the remaining fingers equally.

Moderately slow to Moderately fast

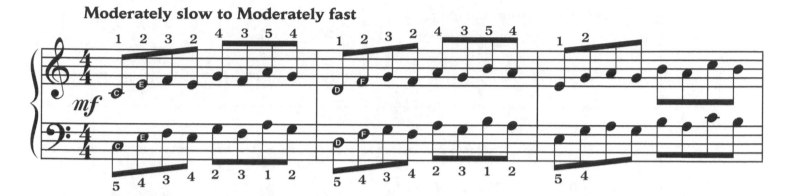

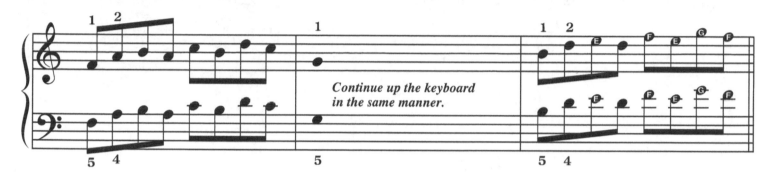

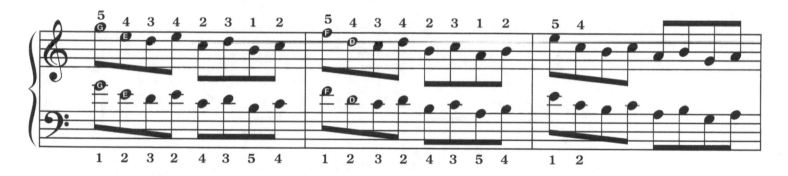

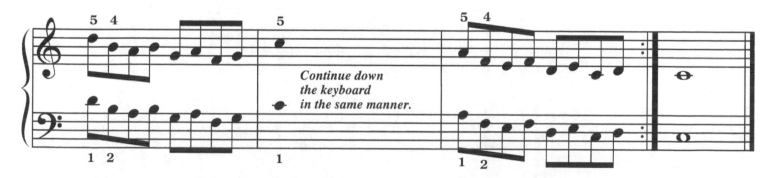

After you have learned to play No. 1 & 2 evenly, at a moderate speed, you may also benefit by practicing them softly, with the fingers close to the keys. On the repeat, play very loudly, lifting the fingers very high. It is also good to begin each exercise softly, making a gradual *crescendo* as you go higher, then gradually *diminuendo* as you come down again to the lowest notes. This builds great control of each finger muscle.

Dotted Quarter Notes

A dot increases the length of a note by *one half its value.*

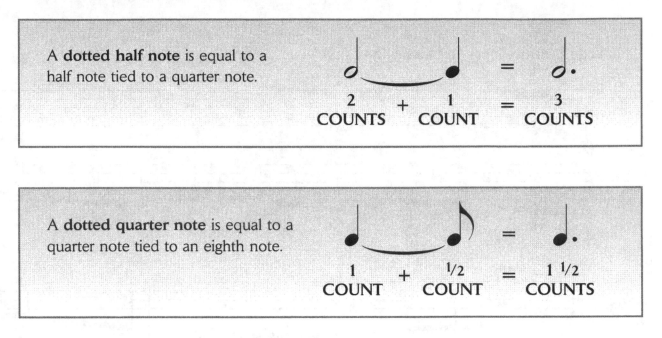

A **dotted half note** is equal to a half note tied to a quarter note.

$$\begin{array}{ccccc} & & & = & \\ \underset{\text{COUNTS}}{2} & + & \underset{\text{COUNT}}{1} & = & \underset{\text{COUNTS}}{3} \end{array}$$

A **dotted quarter note** is equal to a quarter note tied to an eighth note.

$$\begin{array}{ccccc} & & & = & \\ \underset{\text{COUNT}}{1} & + & \underset{\text{COUNT}}{^1/_2} & = & \underset{\text{COUNTS}}{1\,^1/_2} \end{array}$$

Rhythm Exercise: Away from the Keyboard

Clap (or tap) the following rhythm. Clap *once* for each note, counting aloud.

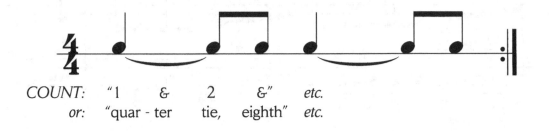

COUNT: "1   &   2   &"   etc.
or: "quar - ter   tie,   eighth"   etc.

The only difference between the following measure and the one above is the way they are written. They are played the same.

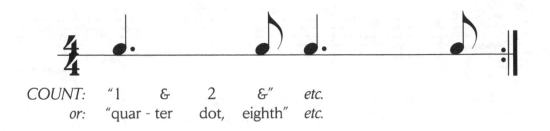

COUNT: "1   &   2   &"   etc.
or: "quar - ter   dot,   eighth"   etc.

In 4/4 or 3/4 time, the dotted quarter note is almost *always* followed by an eighth note!

Measures from Familiar Songs Using Dotted Quarter Notes

1. Clap (or tap) & count.

2. Play & count.

3. Play & sing the words.

C Position

Si - lent night, Ho - ly night,

Middle C Position (Both thumbs on Middle C)

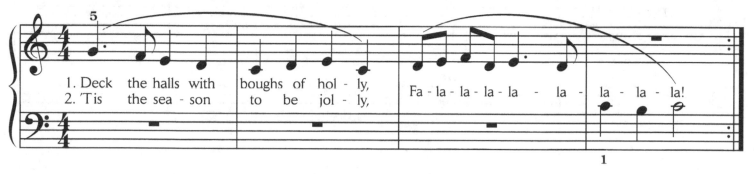

1. Deck the halls with boughs of hol - ly,
2. 'Tis the sea - son to be jol - ly,

Fa - la - la - la - la - la - la - la - la!

Middle C Position

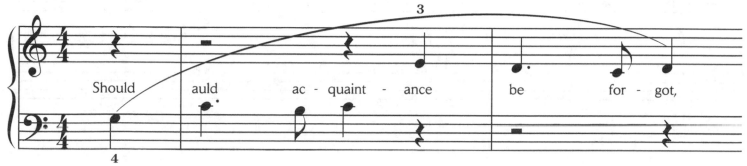

Should auld ac - quaint - ance be for - got,

C Position

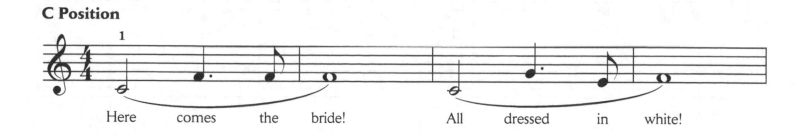

Here comes the bride! All dressed in white!

Alouette

French Folk Song

Brightly

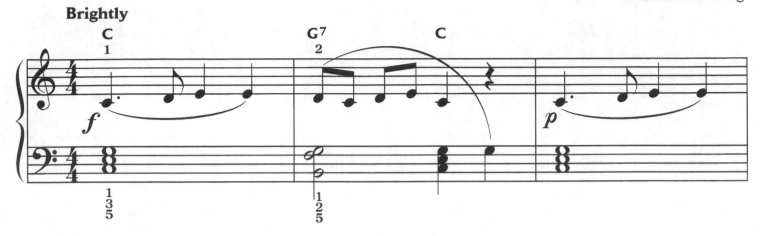

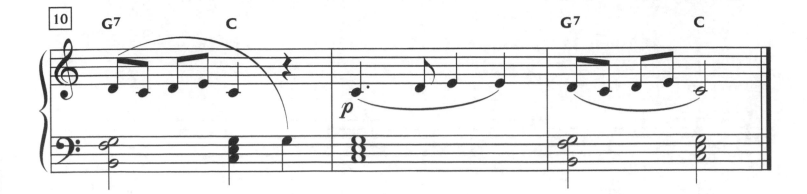

Rhythm Exercise: Away from the Keyboard

Clap (or tap) the following rhythms, counting aloud.

Practice Exercise: Sight Reading

Practice Exercise: Sight Reading

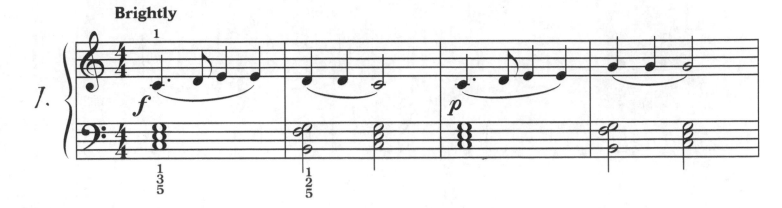

Ach, du lieber Augustine

German Folk Song

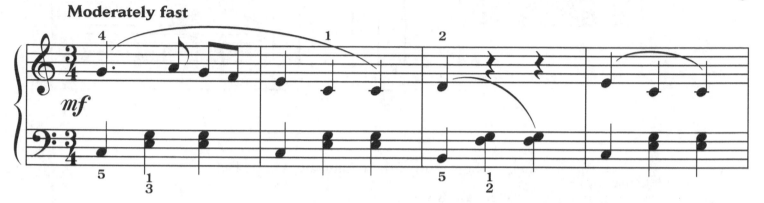

Unit 11

6ths, 7ths and Octaves

6ths

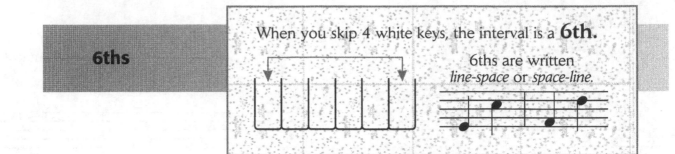

When you skip 4 white keys, the interval is a **6th.**

6ths are written
line-space or *space-line.*

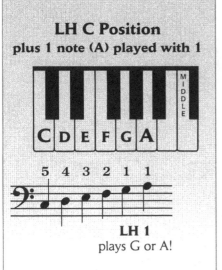

RH C Position
plus 1 note (A) played with 5

C D E F G A
1 2 3 4 5 5

RH 5
plays G or A!

Say the names of these intervals as you play!

Melodic Intervals

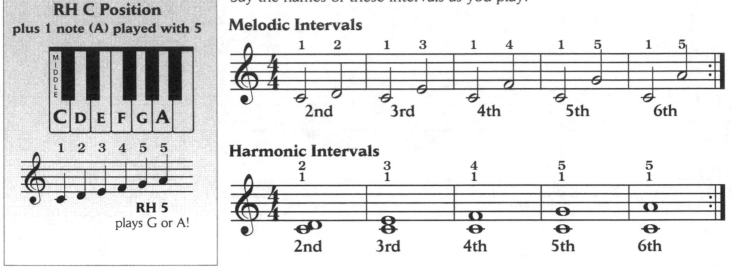

2nd   3rd   4th   5th   6th

Harmonic Intervals

2nd   3rd   4th   5th   6th

LH C Position
plus 1 note (A) played with 1

C D E F G A
5 4 3 2 1 1

LH 1
plays G or A!

Say the names of these intervals as you play!

Melodic Intervals

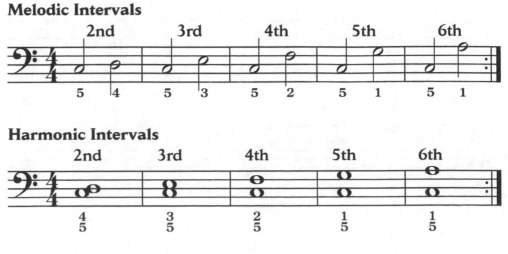

2nd   3rd   4th   5th   6th

Harmonic Intervals

2nd   3rd   4th   5th   6th

Technic Exercise: Warm-Up

In *Lavender's Blue,* 5ths and 6ths are played with 1 & 5. Practice this warm-up before playing *Lavender's Blue.*

Lavender's Blue

C Position + 1

Moderately fast

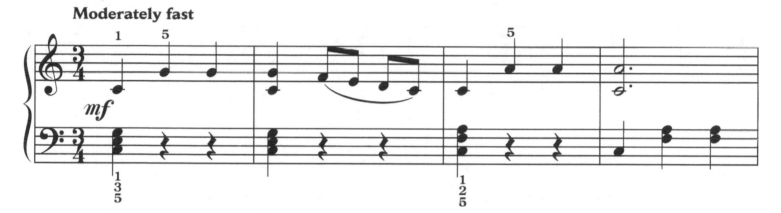

6ths are written *line-space* or *space-line*.

up a 6th   *down* a 6th

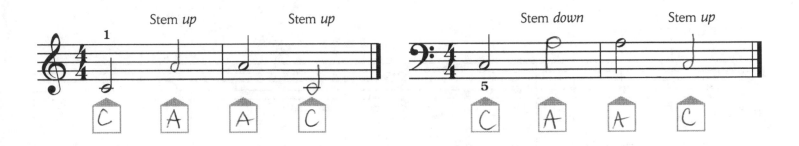

Write and Play Exercise

1. On the staffs below, write a half note *up* a 6th from each C and *down* a 6th from each A.

2. Write the name of each note in the square below it—then play and say the note names.

Stem *up*   Stem *up*   Stem *down*   Stem *up*

C   A   A   C   C   A   A   C

3. Write a whole note *above* the given note in each measure below to make the indicated harmonic interval.

4. Write the names of the notes in the squares. Write the name of the lower note in the lower square; the name of the higher note in the higher square.

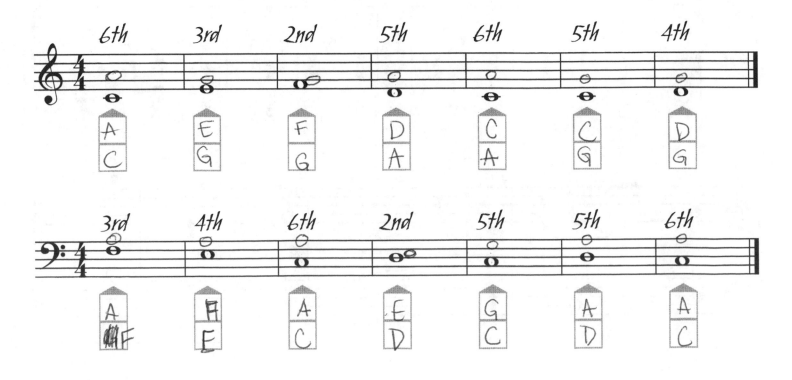

6th 3rd 2nd 5th 6th 5th 4th

A   E   F   D   C   C   D
C   G   G   A   A   G   G

3rd 4th 6th 2nd 5th 5th 6th

A   F   A   E   G   A   A
F   E   C   D   C   D   C

New Time Signature

$\begin{smallmatrix}2\\4\end{smallmatrix}$ means 2 beats to each measure.
$\begin{smallmatrix}2\\4\end{smallmatrix}$ means a quarter note ♩ gets one beat.

Kum-ba-yah!

(with Changing Time Signatures)

COUNT: 1   1   1 – 2
or: 1   2   1 – 2

Moderately slow

mf 1. Kum – ba yah, my Lord, Kum ba – yah!
2. Some – one's pray – ing, Lord, Kum ba – yah!

COUNT: 1 & 2 & 1 & 2 & 3 & 4 &

Kum – ba yah, my Lord, Kum ba – yah!
Some – one's pray – ing, Lord, Kum ba – yah!

Kum – ba yah, my Lord, Kum ba – yah!
Some – one's pray – ing, Lord, Kum ba – yah!

Oh, Lord, Kum ba – yah!
Oh, Lord, Kum ba – yah!

Kum-ba-yah means "come by here."

Written Exercise: Away from the Keyboard

1. Connect the dots on the matching boxes.

2. Write the interval name (2, 3, 4, 5 or 6) on the line.

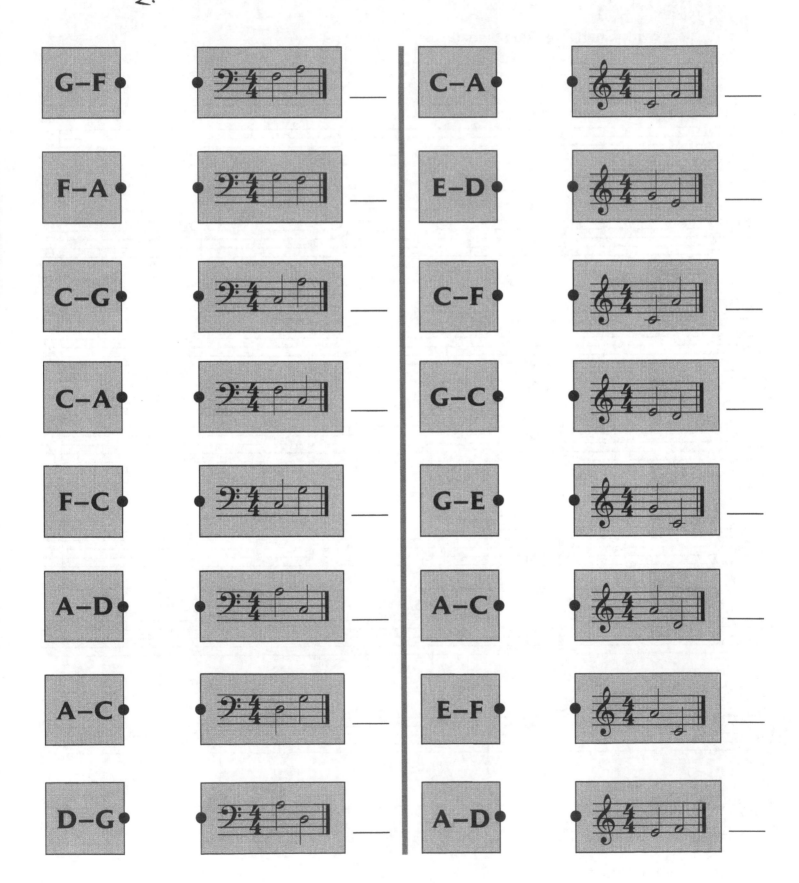

London Bridge

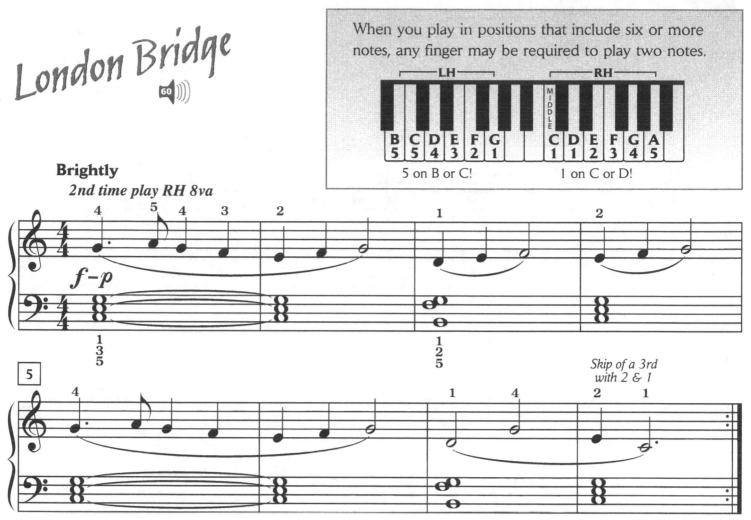

When you play in positions that include six or more notes, any finger may be required to play two notes.

5 on B or C!   1 on C or D!

Brightly
2nd time play RH 8va

f–p

*Skip of a 3rd
with 2 & 1*

Michael, Row the Boat Ashore

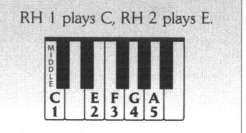

RH 1 plays C, RH 2 plays E.

Moderately slow
2nd time play RH 8va

p–f

Practice Exercise: Sight Reading

Brightly

1.

5

Moderately slow

2.

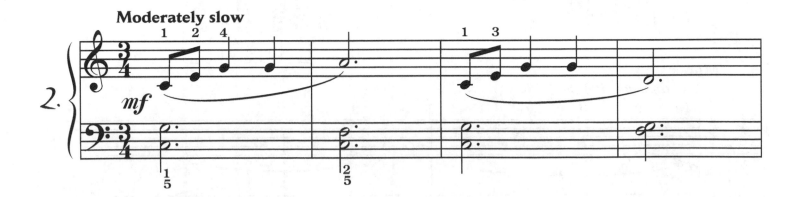

5

Blow the Man Down!

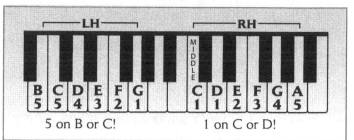

5 on B or C!   1 on C or D!

Moderately fast

Come all ye young fel - lows who fol - low the

sea, Sing - ing "Way! Hey! Blow the man

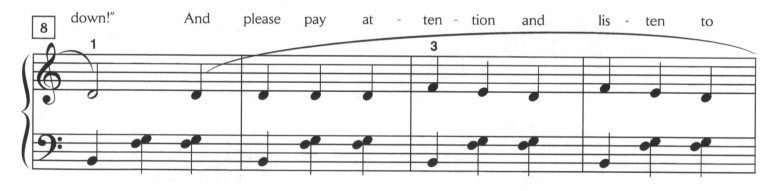

down!" And please pay at - ten - tion and lis - ten to

me; Give us some time to blow the man down!

ritardando

Moving Up and Down the Keyboard in 6ths

To play popular and classical music, you must be able to move freely over the keyboard. These exercises will prepare you to do this. Each hand plays 6ths, moving up and down the keyboard to neighboring keys. *Read only the lowest note of each interval,* adding a 6th above!

RH 6ths, MOVING FROM A/C **UP TO** E/G **AND BACK.**

Begin with RH 1 on middle C.

LH 6ths, MOVING FROM C/E **DOWN TO** F/A **AND BACK.**

Begin with LH 1 on middle C.

Staccato

The dot over or under a note indicates the **staccato** touch. Make these notes very short!

Lone Star Waltz

This piece combines the positions used in *London Bridge* with *Moving Up & Down the Keyboard in 6ths.*

Moderate waltz tempo
2nd time both hands 8va

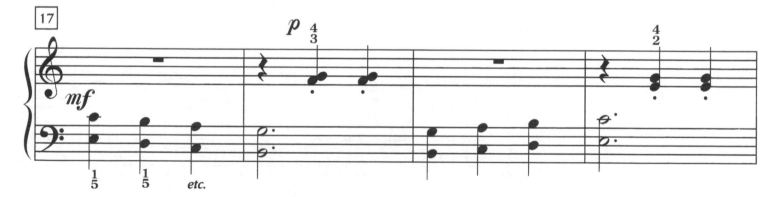

D. C. al Fine

Practice Exercise: Sight Reading

Moderate waltz tempo

Hanon's Aerobic Sixths

Notice how cleverly Hanon uses the interval of a 6th to raise the hands to the next higher position, then to lower them back again.

Lift fingers high. Play each note clearly and distinctly. Practice slowly, then gradually increase speed.

Moderately slow to Moderately fast

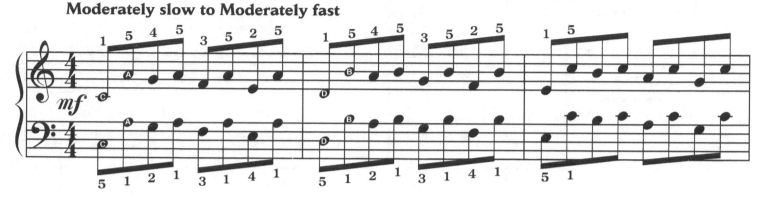

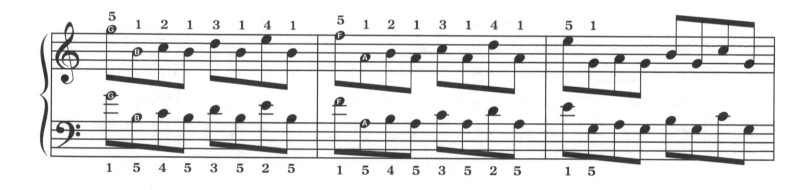

*Continue up the keyboard
in the same manner.*

*Continue down
the keyboard
in the same manner.*

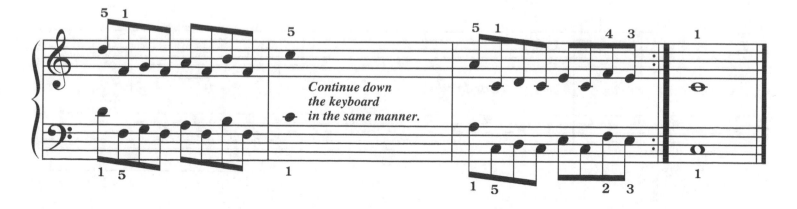

The RH plays only harmonic 6ths (except in measure 16).
You need only read the lowest note of each interval, adding
a 6th above.

The LH uses two different broken-chord accompaniment styles.

Alice Hawthorne

Written Exercise: Away from the Keyboard

1. Connect the dots on the matching boxes.

2. Write the interval name (2, 3, 4, 5 or 6) on the line.

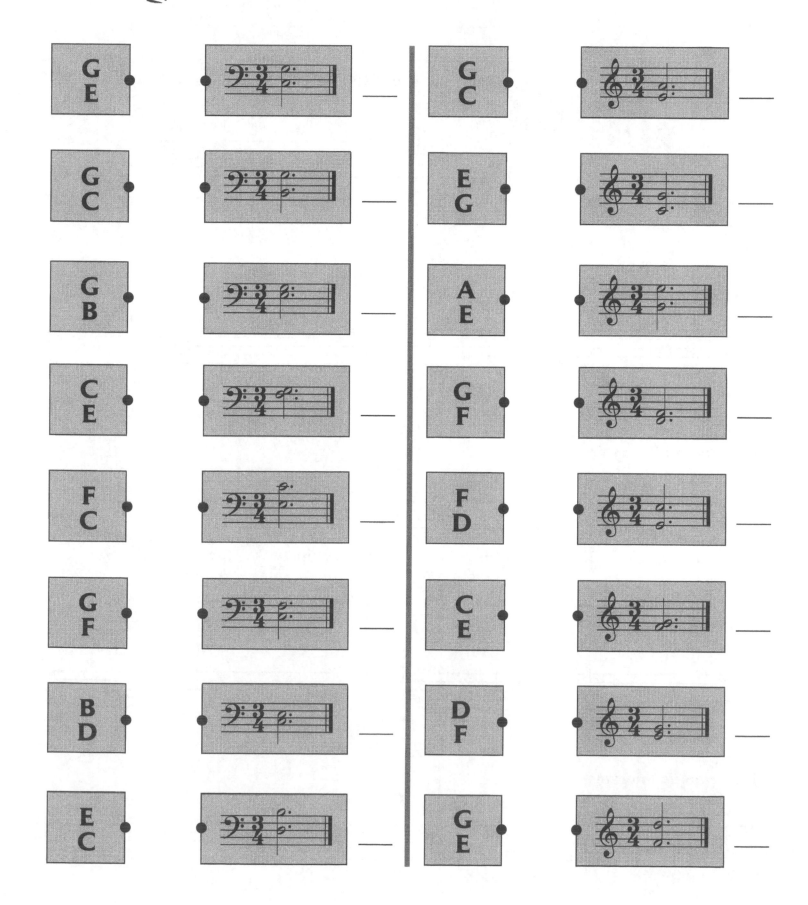

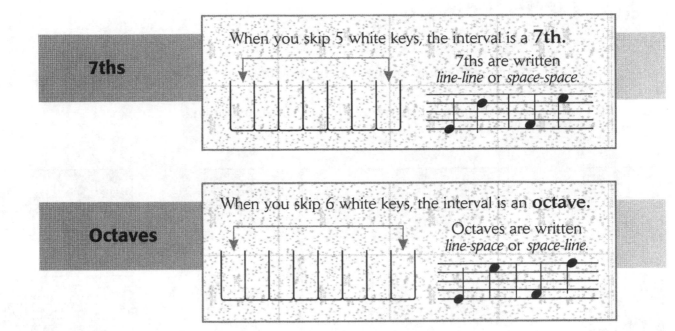

7ths

When you skip 5 white keys, the interval is a **7th.**

7ths are written
line-line or *space-space.*

Octaves

When you skip 6 white keys, the interval is an **octave.**

Octaves are written
line-space or *space-line.*

Say the names of these intervals as you play!

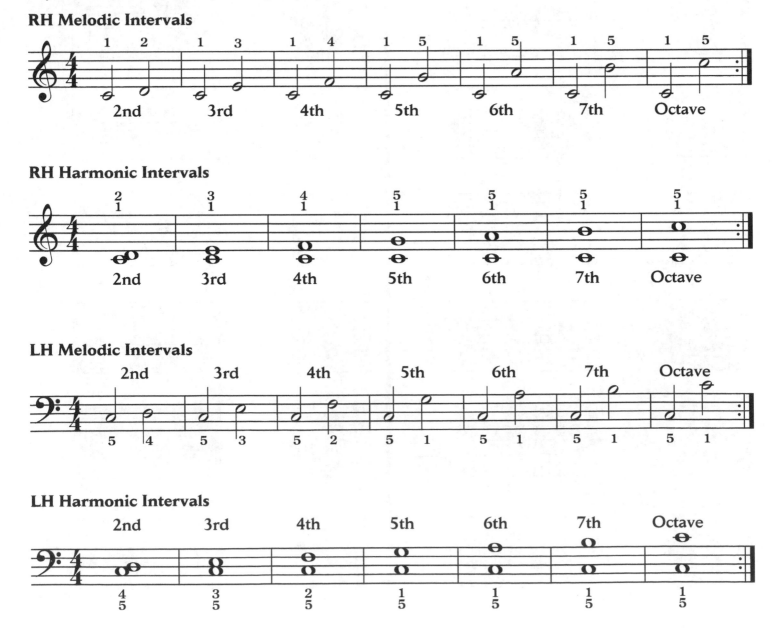

RH Melodic Intervals

RH Harmonic Intervals

LH Melodic Intervals

LH Harmonic Intervals

Practice Exercise: **Sight Reading**

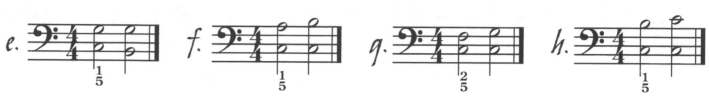

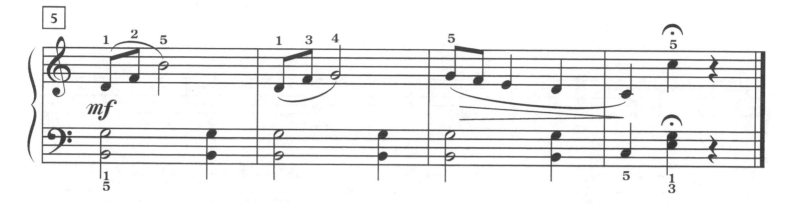

Café Vienna

Play hands separately at first, then together. Be especially careful of the RH fingering! Notice that the first two notes, a melodic 3rd, are played with 2 & 1.

Moderate waltz tempo

Lullaby

Brahms was interested in folk music throughout his life.
The melody of his familiar "Lullaby," one of nearly 200
songs that he composed, is folk-like although it is not
based on an actual folk song.

Johannes Brahms
(1833–1897)

Moderately

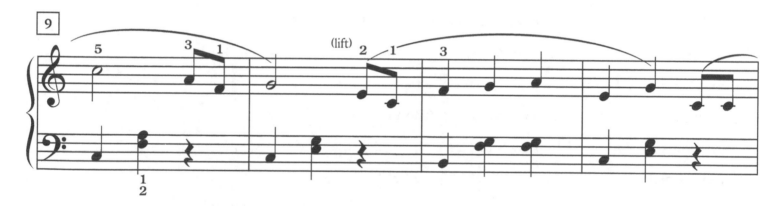

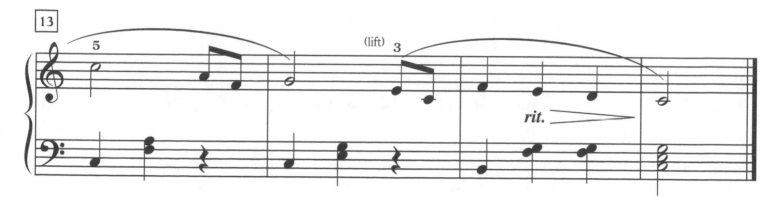

Index

Glossary of Terms & Symbols

Includes all the terms and symbols used in Book 1,
and the page(s) on which they are introduced.

Bar lines Divide music into measures (p. 14).

Bass clef sign ($\mathcal{9}$:) Helps identify notes below middle C; locates the F below the middle of the keyboard (pp. 32, 34).

Block chord When the notes of a chord are played together (p. 100).

Broken chord When the notes of a chord are played separately (pp. 100, 108).

C major chord C E G, G C E (pp. 60, 64, 68, 78, 82, 106, 110).

C position LH 5 on the C below middle C; RH 1 on middle C (pp. 28, 29, 36).

Chord symbol Used to identify chord names (pp. 64, 66).

Chord When three or more notes are played together (p. 60).

Crescendo ($\diagdown$) A dynamic sign that means to play gradually louder (p. 55).

D. C. al Fine (Da Capo al Fine) Means repeat from the beginning and play to the end (Fine) (p. 121).

D^7 chord F♯ C D (pp. 96, 100).

Damper pedal The right pedal. When held down, any tone you sound will continue after you release the key (pp. 12, 104).

Diminuendo ($\diagup$) A dynamic sign that means to play gradually softer (p. 55).

Dotted half note ($\downarrow$.) Receives 3 counts in $\frac{3}{4}$ and $\frac{4}{4}$ time (p. 22).

Dotted quarter note ($\downarrow$.) Equal to a quarter note tied to an eighth note (p. 126).

Double bar line (‖) Used at the end of a piece (p. 14).

Dynamic signs Tell how loud or soft to play (pp. 11, 55).

Eighth notes ($\downarrow\downarrow$) Two eighth notes are played in the time of one quarter note (p. 119).

F major chord F A C, C F A (pp. 78, 82).

Fermata Hold the note under the fermata longer than its value (p. 118).

Fifth (5th) When you skip three white keys. 5ths are written line-line or space-space (p. 47).

Fine End (p. 121).

Flat sign (♭) Play the next key to the left, whether black or white (p. 114).

Forte (f) Loud (p. 11).

Fourth (4th) When you skip two white keys. 4ths are written line-space or space-line (p. 46).

G major chord	G B D (pp. 96, 100, 106, 110).
G position	LH 5 on the G below middle C; RH 1 on the G above middle C (p. 88).
G⁷ chord	B F G (pp. 64, 68).
Grand staff	The bass staff and the treble staff joined together by a brace (p. 36).
Half note (♩)	Receives 2 counts in ¾ and ⁴⁄₄ time (p. 16).
Half rest (▬)	A sign of silence for the value of a half note (p. 17).
Harmonic interval	The distance between two tones that are played together (p. 44).
Incomplete measure	A measure at the beginning of a piece with fewer counts than indicated in the time signature (p. 81).
Legato	To smoothly connect two or more notes (p. 73).
Leger line	A short line added above or below the staff to extend its range (pp. 35, 36).
Line note	A note written on a line (p. 33).
Measure	The area between two bar lines. Bar lines divide the music into measures of equal duration (p. 14).
Melodic interval	The distance between two tones that are played separately (p. 40).
Mezzo forte (*mf*)	Moderately loud (p. 11).
Middle C	The C nearest the middle of the piano (p. 20).
Middle C position	Both thumbs are on middle C (p. 54).
N.C. (no chord)	Means to play no chord (p. 99).
Notes	The symbols on the staff that indicate pitch and duration of tones (p. 14).
Octave	Eight notes, or the interval of an 8th (when you skip 6 white keys). Octaves are written line-space or space-line (pp. 72, 91, 112, 117, 146).
Phrase	A musical thought or sentence (p. 73).
Piano (*p*)	Soft (p. 11).
Quarter note (♩)	Receives 1 count in ¾ and ⁴⁄₄ time (p. 14).
Quarter rest (𝄽)	A sign of silence for the value of a quarter note (p. 15).
Repeat sign (𝄇)	Repeat from the beginning (p. 39).
Repeated notes	Consecutive notes on the same line or space (p. 38).
Rest	A sign of silence (p. 15).
Rhythm	The combining of notes into patterns (p. 14).
Ritardando (rit.)	Gradually slowing (p. 122, 123).

Second (2nd) — The distance from any white key to the next white key. 2nds are written line-space or space-line (p. 40).

Seventh (7th) — When you skip five white keys. 7ths are written line-line or space-space (p. 146).

Sharp sign (♯) — Play the next key to the right, whether black or white (p. 92).

Sixth (6th) — When you skip four white keys. 6ths are written line-space or space-line (p. 132).

Slur — A curved line over or under notes on different lines or spaces; means to play legato (p. 73).

Space note — A note written in a space (p. 33).

Staccato (♩ ♩) — The dot over or under a note. Play the note very short (p. 140).

Staff — The five lines and four spaces on which music is written (p. 32).

Skip (3rd) — Moving up or down from a line to the next line, or from a space to the next space (p. 39).

Step (2nd) — Moving up or down from a line to the next space, or from a space to the next line (p. 38).

Tempo — Speed. Tells how fast or slow to play the music (p. 85).

Third (3rd) — When you skip a white key. 3rds are written line-line or space-space (p. 41).

Tied notes — When notes on the same line or space are joined with a curved line. The key is held down for the combined values of both notes (p. 66).

Time signature ($\frac{4}{4}$, $\frac{3}{4}$, $\frac{2}{4}$) — Numbers that appear at the beginning of music. The top number tells the number of beats (counts) in each measure; the bottom number tells the kind of note that gets 1 beat (pp. 27, 72, 135).

Treble clef sign (𝄞) — Helps identify notes above middle C; locates the G above the middle of the keyboard (pp. 32, 35).

Whole note (o) — Receives 4 counts in $\frac{4}{4}$ time (p. 24).

Whole rest (▬) — A sign of silence for the value of a whole note or for one whole measure (p. 24).